A TRADITION OF POETRY

Sir Philip Sidney and the English Renaissance
Elizabethan Taste

———————

Poems of Michael Drayton
Poems of Charles Cotton

The Earl of Surrey

A
TRADITION
OF
POETRY

JOHN BUXTON

MACMILLAN
LONDON · MELBOURNE · TORONTO
ST MARTIN'S PRESS
NEW YORK
1967

© John Buxton 1967

MACMILLAN AND COMPANY LIMITED
Little Essex Street London WC2
also Bombay Calcutta Madras Melbourne

THE MACMILLAN COMPANY OF CANADA LIMITED
70 Bond Street Toronto 2

ST MARTIN'S PRESS INC
175 Fifth Avenue New York NY 10010

Library of Congress catalog card no. 67-13753

PRINTED IN GREAT BRITAIN
BY R. & R. CLARK LTD., EDINBURGH

CONTENTS

ILLUSTRATIONS

PREFACE

IN the two centuries during which the eight poets with whom this book is concerned were writing poets were not thought of as men set apart from their fellows. Any educated man, anyone who hoped to play some part in the life of his generation as lawyer or soldier, priest or politician, ambassador or magistrate, anyone (in fine) whose company would not be shunned by his fellows, would think it quite natural to try his hand on occasion at a copy of verses. As Sir Thomas Hoby, translating Castiglione, put it : 'it happeneth very seldom that a man not exercised in writing can at any time taste of the sweetness and excellency of styles'. It was not then thought necessary to justify the acquirement of a taste for good literature. You composed a sonnet in Petrarch's manner, or Surrey's, the better to appreciate Petrarch or Surrey ; but in doing so you might discover a talent for writing sonnets, and you would show them to your friends for their opinion. Thus the writing of poetry was part of a social tradition, of the courtier in the sixteenth century, of the complete gentleman in the seventeenth. Six of the poets of whom I have here written were brought up in this tradition ; the other two, Michael Drayton and Lady Winchilsea, deliberately claimed it for themselves. The son of a tanner in a Warwickshire village learnt of the tradition as a child and begged his tutor, in the house of a local squire, to make him a poet. The Maid of Honour to Mary of Modena refused to regard the tradition as exclusively masculine.

These poets were writing in the two centuries when those twin motives of the Renaissance, the wish to follow a European (and therefore classical) tradition, and the wish to assert a native independence (which in vernacular literature is inescapable), were seen not as conflicting but as complementary. John Skelton, who was still writing when Wyatt began to write, rejected the new-fangled classicism with contempt. Pope, writing just before Lady Winchilsea died, was so oppressed by the weight of classical tradition that he called in question the whole English literary achievement of these two hundred years. More or less midway between Skelton and Pope came the great Elizabethans, Sidney and Spenser, Marlowe and Shakespeare, Hooker and Ralegh, who wrote with supreme confidence in the qualities of the English language, at the moment when classical tradition and English independence were in balance.

In literary history, W. P. Ker once said, 'the great difficulty is to give the proper amount of attention to the fashion, the tradition, the school, on the one hand, and on the other to the individual genius'. A few years earlier T. S. Eliot, in an essay on *Tradition and the Individual Talent*, had touched on the same subject. Here, in these studies of eight poets of the sixteenth and seventeenth centuries, I have tried to show them responding in their different ways to the social tradition which recognized poetry as an accomplishment suitable for a gentleman, and to the literary tradition which ran in parallel. In this the name of Horace constantly recurs, and half-way through the period Ben Jonson, by modelling his poetry on Horace's familiar, epistolary style provided the means by which the 'mob of gentlemen' were (to Pope's envy) enabled to write with ease. But the process had begun long before Jonson, and it continued after the Sons of Ben had followed him to the grave. In their different ways these eight poets were responding to the same traditions, making what they could of them in accordance with their own temperament or experience, shaping English diction and syntax and metre to new demands. It is the variety of their response rather than the uniformity of tradition that makes their poetry still worth reading, and these essays are not chapters in a history of the influence of something or other on English poetry but studies of the work of individual poets.

The omission of a portrait of Lady Winchilsea from the illustrations is not an act of wanton misogyny. There were once at least three portraits of her, which were mentioned in her husband's will : an unfinished oil by Riley, who worked in Lely's studio, and two miniatures, one by C. F. Zincke and the other by Laurence Crosse. The last was in existence as recently as 1889 when it was exhibited at Burlington House. It was then the property of Jeffery Whitehead, and it seems all too possible that it may have lost its attribution when his collection was dispersed in 1915. The other two have vanished completely. It is perhaps curious that no engraving of her appears to have survived despite the popularity of her poems, but such appears to be the case.

Six of these essays are revised from briefer studies published elsewhere : in *The Times Literary Supplement* (Wyatt, Surrey, Fanshawe), in the now defunct *Life and Letters* (Lady Winchilsea), and as introductions to my Muses' Library editions of the Poems of Michael Drayton and of Charles Cotton. I am grateful for permission to use again some parts of those studies.

I also wish to thank Mr D. G. Neill for generously allowing me to read and to quote from his unpublished thesis on Lady Winchilsea's Poems ; the Rev. P. Starnes for information about Eastwell Church ; and Mrs Banham, who typed out most of the book from my much corrected manuscript.

August 1966   J. B.

I

SIR THOMAS WYATT

SIR THOMAS WYATT, the son of a Yorkshire squire who had prospered through his loyalty to the Tudor cause, was both an English country gentleman and a Renaissance courtier. He was born in 1503 at Allington Castle in Kent, which the King had granted to his father in 1492, and by the time he was twenty he was already assisting his father in the management of the royal finances. Next year he received his first official appointment as clerk of the King's Jewels, and from that time on he served King Henry VIII chiefly in diplomacy, a career which took him several times to France, and to Italy, Spain, and Portugal, where he became aware of the new fashions in vernacular literature which he was the first to introduce into English. He was a courtier on Castiglione's model — one who could serve his prince with distinction in affairs of state, but also a man of cultivated taste and intellectual accomplishment. He had, it was said, 'as much wit to mark and remember everything he seeth as any young man in England', but also, having travelled into Italy, he 'greatly polished our rude and homely manner of vulgar poesy from that it had been before'. He was thus doubly acceptable to a King whose ambition it was to make his English court rival those of Francis I and other Renaissance princes of Europe. Henry VIII encouraged artists and scholars to come to England, and though Michelangelo declined his invitation Holbein accepted it, and while he was here painted Wyatt's portrait. The King himself was a gifted musician, who also wrote courtly lyrics for singing ; he must have rejoiced to have among his courtiers one who could translate and transpose into English the Italian forms of sonnet, *strambotto* and *terza rima*, and the French *rondeau*, and thereby demonstrate that the English language, which his old tutor Skelton was still using with crude vigour, was malleable to the new elegance. These were the qualities for which the Elizabethans especially valued Wyatt, for they too wished to show that English poetry could rival Italian or French. Consequently they saw little difference between the poetry of Wyatt and Surrey, which they read in Tottel's anthology; but on the whole they preferred, and rightly preferred, Surrey, who was the more polished poet, and better at writing the kind of poetry they themselves wished to write.

Wyatt could not wear the new fashions with the aristocratic grace that came naturally to Surrey. They looked too lately borrowed, and ill suited the sturdy figure of an English squire, which at heart Wyatt remained. In the first satire he confesses to his friend John Poynz that he has always been happier on his country estate than at Court, that he prefers the company he finds there :

> *It is not for because I scorn or mock*
> *The power of them to whom fortune hath lent*
> *Charge over us, of right, to strike the stroke :*
> *But true it is that I have always meant*
> *Less to esteem them than the common sort.*

Not many courtiers preferred, or, at any rate, admitted to preferring 'the common sort'. And towards the end of the same poem Wyatt declares his preference for the simple life at home,

> *to hunt and to hawk*
> *And in foul weather at my book to sit ;*
> *In frost and snow then with my bow to stalk.*
> *No man doth mark where so I ride or go.*

The candour is reinforced rather than diminished by a comparison of these lines with the corresponding lines in Alamanni's tenth satire, on which the poem is modelled. At the end of the poem, where Alamanni says, 'I am in Provence, with my Muses, in a solitary place', Wyatt uses a homely English proverb :

> *But here I am in Kent and Christendom*
> *Among the Muses where I read and rhyme.*

For, as Thomas Nashe tells us, 'William the Conqueror, having heard the proverb of Kent and Christendom, thought he had won a country as good as all Christendom when he was enfeoffed of Kent'. The proverb is obsolete now but it was current among the common sort in the sixteenth century.

How very English this is, this longing to get away from the cares of politics to life at home in the country ! Wyatt would have sympathized with Sir Edward Grey, three and a half centuries later, hoping that electoral defeat would return him to his fishing cottage on the Itchen, to his ducks at Fallodon, and the wild birds on the Northumbrian moors. 'Of course I did my part too as well as I could :', Grey wrote to a friend, 'it would have been shameful not to have done it, but all the same a glorious opportunity of being set free has failed to come off.' Grey too longed for the solitude that Wyatt enjoyed ; and, like Lord Falkland, who pitied unlearned gentlemen on a rainy day, they both took pleasure at being confined indoors by foul weather with a book to read. Yet the sense of duty that drove them all to serve their country without thought of self was no less English.

Wyatt probably began his career as a poet, like Robert Burns, by reworking old popular songs, or by writing new words to existing tunes, before ever he visited the Continent. 'Ah Robin, jolly Robin', the song which Feste sings in *Twelfth Night*, must be one of the earliest, for there is a setting of it by William Cornish, who died in 1523. 'I love loved and so doth she' is another reworking of an old song: there is a setting by Robert Fairfax, who died in 1529. 'I must go walk the woods so wild' is a third such, of which the original version dates from the fifteenth century. Wyatt learnt these songs at home, hearing his father's men singing them of an evening, and polished them up for his sophisticated friends at Court.

Among these from early days, perhaps from childhood, was Anne Boleyn, who was four years younger than Wyatt. They must have seen each other frequently at Court from about 1520, the year of Wyatt's marriage to Elizabeth Brooke, daughter of Lord Cobham. That marriage soon broke up owing to Elizabeth Wyatt's unfaithfulness, and by about 1525 Wyatt and Anne Boleyn had become lovers. A poem which Tottel entitled 'Of his love called Anna' no doubt belongs to the early days of their relationship. The 'word that changeth not though it be turned and made in twain' is the simple palindrome ANNA ; and the third line 'It is mine answer', puns on her name (It is mine Anne, sir) in a similarly light-hearted way. Another poem quotes Anne's motto 'Me and mine'. Two others,

That time that mirth did steer my ship,

and

The knot which first my heart did strain,

are closely linked together, and George Wyatt, the poet's grandson, who wrote a life of Anne Boleyn, said that the second of these referred to her. There is no need to doubt

4

him. In these poems Wyatt was writing in the tradition of courtly love, the stricken lover addressing his cruel mistress, which the King not long afterwards would be using in his letters to Anne. For the love affair which these poems celebrate was soon to end. By the summer of 1527 Anne had become the mistress of the King; and, more than that, the King was determined to marry her as soon as he could obtain a divorce from Queen Catherine. At this point Wyatt, with his usual courage, informed the King that Anne had been *his* mistress, and that she was no fit bride for a King. The King's infatuation with Anne was such that he neither resented this gratuitous piece of information, nor paid much attention to it at the time.

However, Wyatt could no longer continue his liaison with Anne, and for much of the next five years he was on the Continent, first of all in Italy and later in France. As he said in a poem written when Henry and Anne Boleyn came to Calais (where he was serving as Marshal) in October 1532, he fled the fire that had burnt him. It was safer, as well as pleasanter, to be out of the way. In Italy he was taken prisoner by Spanish troops — it was the year of the Sack of Rome — but contrived to escape while his ransom was under negotiation. About this time he adapted one of Petrarch's sonnets to his new situation. Petrarch had referred to the story of Caesar setting free his deer, with a collar to warn other men against molesting them. King Henry on the contrary was claiming his deer for his exclusive possession :

> *graven with diamonds, in letters plain*
> *There is written her fair neck round about :*
> Noli me tangere, *for Caesar's I am.*

And very characteristically Wyatt introduces into this version of an Italian sonnet an English proverb, 'to hold the wind in a net'. A little later he wrote an original sonnet, 'If waker care', in which in the first version he referred to his former love for Anne:

> *since I did refrain*
> *Her that did set our country in a roar.*

But so clear a reference to the controversy over the divorce of Catherine of Aragon, tactless enough at the time, must be toned down in 1536 when the trial and execution of Anne Boleyn had again set the country in a roar. Wyatt therefore revised the lines to read,

> *since I did refrain*
> *Brunet, that set my wealth in such a roar,*

which was harmless enough, since Wyatt's well-being was no man's concern but his own.

Wyatt returned to England late in 1532, and Anne was secretly married early in the new year. On 1 June 1533 the pageants for her coronation took place, in which she was represented by a white falcon. A few days afterwards her vice-chamberlain wrote to a friend to describe the new atmosphere at Court in the summer of 1533. 'As for pastime in the Queen's Chamber, was never more. If any of you that be now departed have any ladies that they thought favoured you, and somewhat would mourn at parting of their servants, I can no whit perceive the same by their dancing and pastime they do use here.' For that company Wyatt, on his return to England from France, wrote many of his poems, more than a hundred of which three ladies of Anne's household — the Duchess of Richmond, who was the poet Surrey's sister, Margaret Douglas, who was the King's niece, and Mary Shelton — collected into a manuscript anthology for their own delectation.

6

Tho: Wiatt Knight.

Sir Thomas Wyatt

These happy days could not last and by the spring of 1536 the King, still anxious for a male heir, was seeking ways to rid himself of Anne. The Queen and her alleged lovers were arrested and imprisoned in the Tower in May, and Wyatt found himself imprisoned there also. He was probably never in danger of execution, but his knowledge of Anne's earlier unchastity might be needed for corroborative evidence, and the King would wish to know where he could be found if need be. In a *strambotto* which alludes to the Queen's badge, 'Lux my fair falcon', and which was most probably written early in May, after her arrest but before his own, Wyatt uses a proverb to comment on those false friends who were now shunning him —

> *they that sometime liked my company,*
> *Like lice away from dead bodies they crawl.*

Not many weeks afterwards, peering through the iron grate of a window in the Tower, Wyatt saw Anne's alleged lovers led out to execution, her brother Lord Rochford, also a poet, and the others, Henry Norris, Francis Weston, William Brereton, whom he must have known well. With them was the musician, Mark Smeaton, who perhaps had sung Wyatt's songs during those nights of pastime in the Queen's Chamber. Well might Wyatt say, turning back from the window after the sad procession had passed,

> *These bloody days have broken my heart,*

and again,

> *The bell tower showed me such sight*
> *That in my head sticks day and night.*

And it is probable that his versions of the Seven Penitential Psalms, poems of repentance for adultery, belong to this time shortly after Anne's execution, which took place two days after her brother's.

How many of Wyatt's poems were written during these brief years when Anne Boleyn was Queen we shall never know, and it is not safe to suppose that Wyatt's heart remained for ever broken by those bloody May days. He was soon back in the King's service as an ambassador, in France, in Spain, in Portugal, but it is not likely that any of Anne's successors gathered about them so congenial a company for which he could write his poems. A few can be dated by historical events to which they refer. Thus 'Of Carthage he, that worthy warrior' alludes to Henry VIII's diplomatic defeat at the hands of the Emperor Charles V and the King of France when they signed the truce of Monzon, 16 November 1537, and thus ended Henry's attempts to play one off against the other by the offer of dynastic marriages. Wyatt saw clearly that Henry had missed the opportunity offered by the death of his Queen, Jane Seymour, a month before, and he expressed himself with unguarded bluntness in the hearing of Edmund Bonner, Bishop of London. 'The King,' Wyatt remarked, 'is left out of the cart's arse, and by God's blood he is well served.' Wyatt's use of the contemporary phrase for missing the bus was noted for future reference by the execrable Bonner.

There are a few other poems written while he was out of England : a version of a poem by Petrarch, in Poulter's measure, addressed to his new mistress Elizabeth Darrell, the melancholy 'What rage is this?' and one or two *strambotti* including his poem of farewell on sailing for home in the summer of 1539,

> *Tagus, farewell, that westward with thy streams*
> *Turns up the grains of gold already tried :*
> *With spur and sail for I go seek the Thames*
> *Gainward the sun, that sheweth her wealthy pride.*

Several of these poems, including this last, exist in Wyatt's own hand in the fair copy of his poems which he kept by him. (For some of the poems are in other hands, but corrected later by the poet; and some, towards the end of the manuscript, entirely in his own.) The last of the poems is a wretched and unfinished paraphrase from a mediaeval astronomical text, the *De Sphaera* of Joannes de Sacrobosco which, as Mr David Scott has shown, Wyatt prepared for celebrating the completion of the astronomical clock now at Hampton Court as part of the welcome to Anne of Cleves. Wyatt left the poem unfinished on returning in November as ambassador to the Court of Charles V. He did not take his manuscript with him.

Fourteen months later Wyatt was again imprisoned in the Tower, this time on a charge of high treason brought against him by Bonner. The spirited speech which he prepared for his defence survives, and in it he turned the tables brilliantly on his accusers, and appealed to those who knew him to agree that he was 'wont sometimes to rap out an oath in earnest talk' and that he was fond of using proverbs. A *strambotto* addressed to his friend and fellow-poet, Sir Francis Brian, 'Sighs are my food, drink are my tears', echoes phrases from the *Defence* and must have been written at this time. But the *Defence* may never have been needed, and by March Wyatt was free once more, and the last and most dangerous crisis of his life was over. Eighteen months later, on his way to the Continent once again, he was taken suddenly ill, and died, and was buried in October 1542 in Sherborne Abbey.

So far I have been concerned with those poems which can be associated with the known facts of Wyatt's life: his relations with Anne Boleyn, his diplomatic missions for the King, his imprisonments in the Tower. I think it is very likely that more of his poems were composed during the years 1533–1536, when Anne was Queen, than during any comparable period of his life. That was the time when he was not employed on diplomatic errands, but was at home in England, and that company would be more appreciative of his poetry than any other. They would delight in his translations and adaptations of Italian and French poems, for the assurance these brought that they were in touch with the latest Continental fashions; but they would also welcome the more polished versions of English songs and carols which Wyatt was so skilled in providing. He would thus refresh their taste for what they already knew, and would make the exotic style of Italian poetry acceptable to them. They would discover in his poems the courtier come from the Courts of Italy and France with news of that more sophisticated world to which they aspired, as well as the English gentleman come up to Court from his estates in the country, whose experience they shared.

Of the two, though they may not have been willing to admit this, the country gentleman was the better poet. A liking for proverbs, and a ready wit in using them, is characteristic not only of Wyatt's verse — certainly it is that — but of a man who preferred the common sort. This was the kind of speech he would hear from his men who accompanied him out hunting or shooting, who worked about his house and his farms. His speech, as we may see from the *Defence*, was naturally racy and colloquial, like that of many another English country gentleman from his day to ours. Most of his friends and fellow-poets among the courtiers would have been too discreet, or too self-conscious, to use such terms, to say that the King had been left out of the cart's arse, or to quote such vulgar proverbs as 'new broom sweeps clean', and 'a rolling stone gathers no moss'. But it is just this quality that gives Wyatt's poetry at its best its unusual vigour.

He knew that this was so. Often he called attention to his use of a proverb with some such phrase as 'after the old proverb', or 'the proverb saith', or 'it is an old saying', or 'as they say' or 'for sure'. There was nothing apologetic about this, and he would introduce his English proverbs into a version of a poem by Petrarch or Serafino as unhesitatingly as into an original poem. His audience would know the proverbs as well as he (even if most were more chary of using them) and they would know the story of the farmer who kissed his cow:

> For fancy ruleth, though right say 'Nay',
> Even as the goodman kissed his cow.

Scott knew it too, and if we have forgotten it, that is our loss.

Wyatt knew, and admitted, that his style was 'somewhat plain', that he had 'a short manner of speech', that his language was 'without eloquence, plain, unpainted and not unknown'. He recognized that this style of his was true to the man he knew himself to be:

> Yet some there be that take delight
> To judge folks' thought for envy and spite,
> But whether they judge me wrong or right,
> I am as I am, and so do I write.

Wyatt's plain style derived from his own personality not, like Ben Jonson's seventy or eighty years afterwards, from a careful study of the familiar epistolary style of Horace; the English tradition of carol and song had more to do with his plainness. Later, when he wrote satire, he found that his own best manner suited his adaptation of Horace's story of the town mouse and the country mouse, but this was due more to luck than learning. For Wyatt as for Ben Jonson this plain style had the advantage of enabling him to say what he wished clearly and succinctly, with a brusque directness far removed from the work of most of his contemporaries.

Ben Jonson wrote his poems out first in prose, as William Camden had taught him to do when he was a schoolboy at Westminster. There is no reason to think that Wyatt did the same, but in many of his best poems he, like Jonson, follows the natural English prose order of words. 'They flee from me that some time did me seek', is an example of this ; so are 'My lute awake', 'Is it possible ?', 'What should I say, since faith is dead', 'I see that chance had chosen me' and 'Quondam was I in my lady's grace'. In other poems the most striking stanzas are effective just for this reason, because no inversion or other literary device stands between the reader and Wyatt. 'Who list his wealth and ease retain' starts conventionally enough until personal misery bursts through in the third and fourth stanzas.

> *These bloody days have broken my heart.*
> *My lust, my youth did then depart*
> *And blind desire of estate.*
> *Who hastes to climb seeks to revert.*
> *Of truth*, circa regna tonat.
>
> *The bell tower showed me such sight*
> *That in my head sticks day and night.*
> *There did I learn out of a grate,*
> *For all favour, glory or might,*
> *That yet*, circa regna tonat.

We are with Wyatt in the Tower, in the spring of 1536.

As we should expect, he achieves this effect in the second satire, which is based on the sixth satire of Horace's second book.

My mother's maids, when they did sew and spin,
They sang some time a song of the field mouse
That, forbecause her livelihood was but thin,
Would needs go seek her townish sister's house.

All is direct, conversational, unforced ; but it was no small feat to do this in the first *terza rima* in English, a metre which few English poets except Shelley* have managed well since.

This same natural easy manner Wyatt can combine, again like Ben Jonson and his Tribe, with an extraordinary gift for writing songs. There is no reason to assume (or, for that matter, not to assume) that he himself could compose and play and sing. But he wrote new words for old songs, or new songs for musicians to set, for himself or his friends to sing in the Queen's Chamber and elsewhere. From the native lyrical tradition he learnt much, and more that was congenial to his own gifts than ever he learnt from the Italians ; he refers to his poems as songs ; he alludes several times to the lute, which would be unusually silly and affected if he did not mean such poems to be sung to the accompaniment of the lute. A poem which begins

My lute awake, perform the last
Labour that thou and I shall waste,

and which ends

Now cease, my lute, this is the last
Labour that thou and I shall waste,
And ended is that we begun.
Now is this song both sung and past.
My lute be still, for I have done,

* And the Countess of Pembroke in her translation of Petrarch's *Trionfo della Morte*, and Byron in *The Prophecy of Dante.*

must surely be, what he calls it, a song. So must many another, including the equally famous

Blame not my lute

for which settings survive in two manuscripts. Such songs were precursors of the ayres which Dowland's virtuosity made famous throughout Europe at the end of the century.

Indeed it is in such songs that Wyatt's best gifts most appear : his forthright, vigorous language ; his metrical versatility ; his sense of what is needed for a good song — clarity, progression, and the recognition that something must be left for the music to supplement. (For, if this is not done, musical setting can only detract from the total effect.) And in these songs Wyatt is writing almost wholly in an English tradition of secular lyric, carol, and ballad, uninfluenced by Italian or French models and careless of them. He was skilled in the use of the refrain, essentially a musical device, whether in the repetition of a simple phrase, 'In eternum', 'Is it possible ?' 'Ah, my heart, ah ! what aileth thee ?' ; or in repetition with variation, as in 'I am as I am, and so shall I be' ; or in the more unusual pattern to be found in 'Heaven and earth and all that hear me plain', where a word or phrase is repeated at the end of each stanza, but a different one in each stanza. (The lute music for this last poem, a version of an English pavan, survives.) These refrains, too, bore Wyatt's imprint, in that he made them out of simple, collo-quial phrases with a direct appeal to the audience — 'There-fore, take heed', 'What meaneth this ?', 'Say nay, say nay', 'Forget not yet', 'Who could have thought so ?' — which was far more effective than the usual decorative refrain.

Thus we come to something of a paradox, that Wyatt, whose significance to his own century lay in the fact that he introduced courtly Renaissance fashions into English poetry, is really at his best when he forgets all this and writes songs in a native, and therefore mediaeval, tradition of lyric. Or, to put this another way, Wyatt the son of a Yorkshire squire who had made good under Henry VII, writes better poetry than Wyatt the astute ambassador from Henry VIII to the Emperor Charles V.

And yet, perhaps, in what we now regard as the best of all his poems these two personalities miraculously fuse and combine.

> They flee from me that some time did me seek
>   With naked foot stalking in my chamber.
> I have seen them gentle, tame and meek
>   That now are wild and do not remember
>   That some time they put themselves in danger
> To take bread at my hand. And now they range
> Busily seeking with a continual change.
>
> Thanked be fortune, it hath been otherwise —
>   Twenty times better; but once in special,
> In thin array after a pleasant guise,
>   When her loose gown from her shoulders did fall,
>   And she me caught in her arms long and small;
> Therewithal sweetly did me kiss
> And softly said, 'Dear heart, how like you this?'
>
> It was no dream. I lay broad waking.
>   But all is turned thorough my gentleness
> Into a strange fashion of forsaking;
>   And I have leave to go, of her goodness,
>   And she also to use newfangledness.
> But since that I so kindly am served,
> I would fain know what she hath deserved.

He is using Troilus rhyme, the rhyme royal stanza of Chaucer's *Troilus and Criseyde*, the masterpiece which derived from Boccaccio's *Teseide* and which the sixteenth century regarded as a heroic poem of the same kind as the *Orlando furioso*. In the first stanza the poet broods on the fickleness of his mistresses, and echoes the words of a fifteenth-century carol which had listed various kinds of women,

> *Sum be wyse, and sum be fonde,*
> *Sum be tame, I understond,*
> *Sum will take bred at a manus hond.*

The movement within the stanza is slow and meditative. All but one of the lines are enjambed ; and there are but three stops. Then, in the second stanza, he remembers that things have not always been so, and he vividly recalls one special occasion when he and she returned together after a Court masque, and, to match the passion of his recollection, the quick, short phrases never flow over from one line to the next, and do not always require even a complete line. In the last stanza he returns to the cold reality of the present, and a mood of cynicism replaces the regret of the first stanza. The recollection of the second stanza is dismissed in two curt phrases in the opening line. Then he blames himself for not having been firm enough ; alludes to the lady's condescending rejection of him, and ironically asks what she deserves. Here, the last six lines are divided into pairs — a third variant on the pattern of the stanza, again perfectly adapted to what the poet has to say. In this, as in all the best of Wyatt's poems, there is the lively, onward flow of good talk ; no hesitation, no seeking after effect, no airs and graces, but Wyatt as he was. And there is also the subtle use of a complex metrical form, the variation of clause length against line length, the essential counterpoint between the rhythms of speech and of verse.

Wyatt's contemporaries and successors found it easier to comment on his introduction of what was alien and exotic than to detect the new life that he had given to what was English and everyday. His experiments with foreign forms distracted him for a time, but in the end his experience of Italian and French and Latin poetry helped him to correct the irregularity and diffuseness which, as he himself acknowledged, had been faults of his earlier poetry. As he told Queen Catherine, he gave up a translation which he had begun for her of Petrarch's *De remediis utriusque fortunae* because he found that 'for lack of such diversity in our tongue it should want a great deal of the grace', recognizing the contrast between Petrarch's brilliance, even in Latin, and his own manner which seemed to him inevitable in English. The new Italian style did not suit him — one of the things he always disliked was new-fangledness — but once assimilated it gave a touch of urbanity to the racy speech of an English country gentleman who might otherwise have sounded slightly provincial. In an English context Wyatt was anything but that, but the ambassador who had served so long on the Continent was conscious of a wider context and so, from being a refurbisher of old songs, came to be our first great lyric poet.

TEXTS

Collected Poems, ed. Kenneth Muir (Muses' Library), Routledge & Kegan Paul, 1949 (and later reprints).
Unpublished Poems from the Blage MS., ed. Kenneth Muir, Liverpool University Press, 1961.

2

THE EARL OF SURREY

HENRY HOWARD, Earl of Surrey, 'that Princely Surrey who was then the prime of England's noble youth', descendant of kings, grandson of the victor of Flodden Field, handsome, dashing, brave, arrogant, and rash, went to the executioner's block a little before his thirtieth birthday, leaving a romantic legend of the lover of Fair Geraldine and a number of poems which, till but the other day, maintained for him a reputation as the greatest English poet between Chaucer and Spenser. The portrait by Guillim Scrots at Arundel Castle shows him in the last year of his life, splendid in embroidered clothes and plumed hat, the Garter about his leg, his right arm resting on a broken column. The elaborate Mannerist surround to his portrait, with semi-nude figures in the Italian style displaying shields of medi-aeval heraldry, is the work of a painter trained in the Habsburg courts ; and this image of an English nobleman in a classical frame is also a portrayal of the Magnificent Man of Renaissance imagination.

Henry VIII had chosen Surrey to be the companion of his bastard son the Duke of Richmond, and together the two boys—Surrey was fifteen, Richmond some eighteen months younger—spent the year 1532 in France at the Court of Francis I. That same year Surrey married Lady Frances Vere, daughter of the Earl of Oxford, and on their return to England in 1533 Richmond married Surrey's sister, Lady

Mary Howard. Thus from early youth Surrey, born heir to the most powerful family in England, one always in danger for its proximity to the Crown, was closely associated with the Court of King Henry.

While in France he travelled about the country with the Court of Francis I, which was self-consciously Italianate. He visited Chantilly and Fontainebleau where he must have seen the architects, sculptors, and painters whom the King had brought to work there busily creating new works of luxurious elegance. There, no doubt, he first learnt of the new attempts to create vernacular literatures on the model of Greece and Rome, first saw portraits such as were later painted of himself, first observed the new classical fashion in architecture, which he would introduce into England in the house called Mount Surrey which he began in 1544 near Norwich, but of which nothing survives. He was never in Italy, though like so many Englishmen, he learnt more from Italian than French poets, and he may have met Alamanni in France. He learnt quickly and precociously, and the impatient energy of his mind, which was often to get him into trouble and would eventually bring him to his death, could penetrate at once beyond the inessential and superficial. His prompt invention of the form of sonnet best suited to English, and his transformation of *versi sciolti* into the first English blank verse are evidence of this. Both experiments proved more important for what they enabled greater poets to achieve fifty years and more after Surrey's death than for what he himself had time to do with them ; but to Sidney and his contemporaries Surrey's poetry, not Wyatt's, seemed especially deserving of praise. The recent rejection of Surrey in favour of Wyatt would have astonished not only the Elizabethans, but the Augustans and Romantics too, and may well be temporary. There were qualities in his poetry which maintained its repute, and which are worth investigating.

The Elizabethans valued Surrey's poetry because Surrey was good at the kind of thing they were trying to achieve, just as we tend to prefer Wyatt because he was better than Surrey at what we attempt. Most poets of the present day would rather have written *They flee from me that some time did me seek* than *When Windsor walls sustained my wearied arm*, but most of our predecessors would have preferred otherwise. There is nothing of the native, and therefore mediaeval, tradition in Surrey's poetry : it is all classical grace and polish. He could write like this :

> *The dewy Iris thus with golden wings*
> *A thousand hues showing against the sun,*
> *Amid the skies then did she fly adown.*

We are at once in Virgil's company, or Marlowe's. Thomas Warton considered that Surrey 'for his justness of thought, correctness of style, and purity of expression, may justly be pronounced the first English classical poet', and commended him therefore to the eighteenth century. Pope, in *Windsor Forest*, paid a double compliment to Surrey and to his patron Lord Lansdowne by calling Surrey 'the Grenville of a former age' ; and he noted that Surrey too found poetic inspiration at Windsor. Pope no less than Puttenham regarded Surrey as one of the first refiners of English poetry. A century later Samuel Rogers set all-accomplished Surrey 'at the head of those who have shed a grace on youth', in this echoing Michael Drayton's praises ; and Hazlitt, by some species of left-wing self-deception, supposed that Leigh Hunt, if he had inherited an estate of £5000 a year, would have been another Surrey.

Warton saw that Surrey's classicism owed more to Latin than to Italian, that he got it direct (so to say) rather than at second hand, characteristically refusing to be content with other men's mediation. Or, to put this another way, his translation from Virgil had more effect on his style than his translations from Italian. (From French, which derived at two removes from Latin, he made but one translation.) The concentration required in making an acceptable version of Virgil in English was necessarily greater than that demanded for translating a modern poet, and this may have helped Surrey to more success than Wyatt in adapting English to his needs. The translator of the *Aeneid* must have richer resources of vocabulary, of syntax, of metre than the translator of a sonnet by Petrarch or a *rondeau* by Clément Marot.

Besides, we must remember that for Surrey's generation, as for Dante's, or Milton's, Virgil was supreme among the world's poets, the Arch-poet, *il poeta*, needing no distinguishing epithet. Therefore to attempt a translation of his masterpiece demanded not only self-confidence such as Surrey evidently possessed, but also confidence in the capacity of the English language to match the Latin in sustaining a poem on the grand scale, together with a sensitivity to the medium which must not fall ludicrously short of Virgil's. That was where the Elizabethan translators, Phaer and Stanyhurst, failed ; and Dryden's deference to Latin led him to underrate 'a language so much inferior' as English. Also, by preferring the couplet to Surrey's blank verse Dryden was the less classical, for Surrey's choice of the form, like Milton's, must have been dictated by a wish to recover ancient liberty to a heroic poem from the troublesome modern bondage of rhyming. Blank verse enabled the poet to use a more complex and flexible syntax to meet the needs of a poem such as the *Aeneid*, so that, again to quote Milton, 'the sense might be variously drawn out from one verse to another'. Dryden, by contrast, used rhyme precisely to 'stop the sense from overflowing into another line'. The translator of Virgil, Dryden believed, must choose between Virgil's complex rhythm and his grace and smoothness, and he chose to sacrifice the rhythm. Surrey denied the necessity for such a choice, or perhaps was unaware of it, and however far he falls short of the extreme sophistication of Virgil's art, at least he represents something of its various qualities.

Blank verse puzzled its first readers. When Surrey's translation of Book IV was published in 1554 the publishers thought it necessary to advertise on the title-page that it was 'drawn into a strange metre'.* Trissino had first used the form in a tragedy, *Sofonisba*, in 1515, and Italian translators of the *Aeneid* had almost at once seen how suitable a medium it might be. In 1534 Niccolò Liburnio used it for a translation of *Aeneid* IV, and Ippolito de' Medici used it for *Aeneid* II in 1539. These were available to Surrey and may have helped to determine his choice of these books to begin with, though almost any poet would be likely to choose the story of Dido and Aeneas in Book IV. Surrey showed his quality not only in preferring *versi sciolti* to English hexameters (such as Stanyhurst attempted) but in naturalizing the metre at once by converting the eleven syllabled Italian line to the ten syllabled English. This acute sensitivity to the possibilities and limitations of his medium is a mark of the greatest artist. Thus Surrey's blank verse is not merely the first but, being the first, it is also very good. The importance of this for those who were to follow needs no emphasis, for an

* Trissino used *versi sciolti* for his heroic poem *Italia liberata dai Gothi*, but this was not published until after Surrey's execution.

unsuccessful experiment with the form might have impeded Marlowe, Shakespeare, and Milton.

How much use Surrey made of Liburnio and Ippolito de'Medici we cannot say. But certainly he had access to the still unpublished Scots version by Gavin Douglas, and made some use of it, while rejecting the rhymed couplet in which Douglas wrote. Comparison of the two versions shows that Surrey's introduction of blank verse had more than prosodic significance. The reader of Gavin Douglas is concerned first and foremost with the narrative, with the subject matter, with what is happening. Douglas is good at describing violent action, and at battle-pieces, which Virgil, like Milton, was not sedulous to indite. He sought to retell a famous story in terms of his own time, lavishly illustrated or encumbered by his own comments and embellishments. The reader of Surrey, like the reader of Milton, or of Virgil, is invited to pay attention to the choice and placing of words; is always on duty. Surrey strove to reproduce the verbal and metrical felicity of a famous poem, and remains himself anonymous and unobtrusive. By this means he demonstrates, for the first time, the capacity of modern English for a poem on this scale, and for the grand manner. As Dryden says, 'We must not only choose our words for elegance, but for sound. To perform which, a mastery of the language is required ; the poet must have a magazine of words, and have the art to manage his few vowels to the best advantage. . . . All which, and a thousand secrets of versification beside, he may learn from Virgil, if he will take him for his guide.' This Surrey, but not Douglas, did. When he wrote it was the manner rather than the matter that needed consideration in English. Roger Ascham, who was Surrey's exact contemporary, put the point well : 'Ye know not what hurt ye do to learning, that care not for words but for matter'.

Virgil uses long, open vowels to represent the melancholy
hooting of an owl :

> *solaque culminibus ferali carmine bubo*
> *saepe queri et longas in fletum ducere voces.*

Douglas's version is this :

> *And oft with wild scryke the nycht owle,*
> *Heich on the rufe, alane, was hard yowle*
> *With langsum voce and a ful petuus beir.*

And Surrey's :

> *And oft the owl with rueful song complained*
> *From the house top, drawing long doleful tunes.*

Douglas, who needs three lines to Virgil's, and Surrey's, two,
produces something not in the least Virgilian, not merely
because of the comparative unfamiliarity of his language, nor
even because, for the sake of the rhyme, his bird must
ignominiously 'yowle', which suggests something comic
rather than sinister. He has entirely missed Virgil's carefully
designed metrical effect, which Surrey skilfully reproduces.

This was a fairly simple task. But Surrey is no less successful with one of Virgil's famous set-pieces, the *Nox erat* of
Book IV, where he displays his exquisite art and virtuosity as
in a cadenza. Surrey accepts the challenge.

> *It was then night ; the sound and quiet sleep*
> *Had through the earth the wearied bodies caught ;*
> *The woods, the raging seas were fallen to rest*
> *When that the stars had half their course declined ;*
> *The fields whist ; beasts and fowls of diverse hue*
> *And what so that in the broad lakes remained*
> *Or yet among the bushy thicks of briar*
> *Laid down to sleep by silence of the night*
> *Gan 'suage their cares, mindless of travails past.*

Here, first, is that subtle variation of clause-length against the rhythmical unit of the line which Virgil used so consummately, and which is one of the surest signs of poetic mastery. So, here, Surrey follows a sentence of three words, 'The fields whist', with one that continues through four and a half lines. In doing so he suggests, as Virgil had suggested, the whole world of living creatures. He emphasizes the silence of the fields by making a long pause after 'whist', and he does so by bringing a heavily stressed syllable to follow another : 'The fields whist ; beasts and fowls . . .'. Insert the definite article here : 'The fields whist ; *the* beasts and fowls . . .', and it is obvious how easily this effect could have been missed, and would have been missed by a lesser poet. Surrey varies the rhythm of his lines ; he draws out the sense from one to another, like Milton ; he manages his vowels to the best advantage, as Dryden advised. In short, he is using his new, strange metre in a mature and self-conscious way so that, even in this famous passage, his lines are not unworthy to stand beside Virgil's.

We may see that Surrey's mastery comes from his attentive and sensitive reading of Virgil himself if we compare his translation of a sonnet which Petrarch derived from these same lines in the *Aeneid*.

> *The beasts, the air, the birds their song do cease ;*
> *The night's car the stars about doth bring ;*
> *Calm is the sea, the waves work less and less.*

Here, for all the felicity of that last line, the passage is much less satisfactory than the direct translation from Virgil. The lines are all end-stopped ; the inversion in the second line (where 'stars' is the subject) is awkward ; and so too is the suggestion, in the first line, that beasts and air may sing like birds.

Yet Surrey, who had an almost Augustan concern with writing well, could learn from Petrarch, and found the Italian manner far more congenial than ever Wyatt did. Both poets made versions of Petrarch's

Amor, che nel penser mio vive e regna,

so that a fair comparison between the two poets may be made. Wyatt presumably wrote first and may be quoted first :

> *The long love, that in my thought doth harbour*
> *And in mine heart doth keep his residence,*
> *Into my face presseth with bold pretence,*
> *And therein campeth, spreading his banner.*
> *She that me learneth to love and suffer,*
> *And wills that my trust and lusts negligence*
> *Be reined by reason, shame and reverence,*
> *With his hardiness taketh displeasure.*
> *Wherewithal, unto the heart's forest he fleeth,*
> *Leaving his enterprise with pain and cry ;*
> *And there him hideth, and not appeareth.*
> *What may I do when my master feareth*
> *But in the field with him to live and die ?*
> *For good is the life ending faithfully.*

And now Surrey :

> *Love that doth reign and live within my thought,*
> *And built his seat within my captive breast,*
> *Clad in the arms wherein with me he fought*
> *Oft in my face he doth his banner rest.*
> *But she that taught me, love and suffer pain,*
> *My doubtful hope and eke my hot desire,*
> *With shamefast look to shadow and refrain,*
> *Her smiling grace converteth straight to ire.*

And coward love then to the heart apace
Taketh his flight, where he doth lurk and plain
His purpose lost, and dare not show his face.
For my lord's guilt thus faultless bide I pain ;
  Yet from my lord shall not my foot remove.
  Sweet is the death that taketh end by love.

Comment is scarcely needed. The difference is not between a good poet and a bad one, but between a poet who has understood Petrarch's art and one who has merely understood the meaning of his words. There is also the difference between one whose natural style was, as Wyatt admitted, 'somewhat plain' (and therefore not readily adaptable for translating Petrarch's elaborate and conceited style), and one whose concern was with literary elegance. Surrey, but not Wyatt, would have approved Gray's dictum that the language of the age is never the language of poetry.

Wyatt's translation of this sonnet is on the Italian pattern, with two rhymes in the octave and three in the sestet. Surrey's is on the English pattern, which he introduced, and which Daniel, Drayton, Shakespeare, and so many other English poets have used. Surrey's invention of this form of the sonnet is further evidence of his precocious sensitivity to language, for it became dominant in English because it is much easier for us to find seven rhymes than five, to have only two words to each rhyme-sound instead of the four with which Wyatt struggles in the octave of his sonnet. This is a fact inherent in the structure of the English language, which Wyatt failed to observe, but which Surrey did. And he had done so by the age of twenty, when, after he had been imprisoned at Windsor for a youthful fracas, he wrote *When Windsor walls*. Already in this poem we can see the characteristic flexibility of rhythm which he gives to his verse by avoiding end-stopped lines. And again, and so soon, there is the delightful counterpoint between syntactical unit and metrical design.

> *When Windsor walls sustained my wearied arm,*
> *My hand my chin, to ease my restless head,*
> *Each pleasant plot revested green with warm,*
> *The blossomed boughs with lusty Ver yspread,*
> *The flowered meads, the wedded birds so late*
> *Mine eye discovered. Then did to mind resort*
> *The jolly woes, the hateless short debate,*
> *The rakehell life that 'longs to love's disport.*
> *Wherewith, alas, mine heavy charge of care*
> *Heaped in my breast brake forth against my will,*
> *And smoky sighs that overcast the air.*
> *My vapoured eyes such dreary tears distil*
>   *The tender Spring to quicken where they fall,*
>   *And I half bent to throw me down withal.*

Here and on other occasions Surrey uses the sonnet for other than love-compliment, for the sort of subject for which hardly any other English poet until Milton would use it. In two sonnets Surrey mourns Sir Thomas Wyatt. In another he commemorates Thomas Clere, who was mortally wounded at the siege of Montreuil in September 1544 while rescuing Surrey, who had himself just been badly wounded. (The sonnet was inscribed on Clere's tomb in the Howard chapel in Lambeth parish church, as Horace Walpole noted, and was perhaps the earliest English poem of any consequence to be so inscribed.) In two other sonnets Surrey adapts famous stories from antiquity in order to make satirical comment on Henry VIII's notorious dissipation. In one of these he wrote, ostensibly, of Sardanapalus, for whom

> *The dent of swords from kisses seemed strange,*
> *And harder than his lady's side his targe ;*
> *From glutton feasts to soldiers' fare a change ;*
> *His helmet far above a garland's charge.*

The compressed, scornful vigour of the phrasing looks forward to Shakespeare's sonnets.

Here perhaps we are to find the answer to those who disparage Surrey by contrast with Wyatt. The romantic insistence that poetry is about poets necessarily promotes those who, like Wyatt, or Donne, may be represented as telling us about their own personal experience, above those who are principally devoted to 'the elegancy, facility, and golden cadence of poetry'. (Shakespeare's admiration for these qualities is capriciously disregarded by those who seek to persuade us that his sonnets are autobiographical.) Wyatt conveys into his verse something of the racy, proverb-studded speech of an English country gentleman, and re-uses phrases from the speech for his defence in 1541 in poems written at the time. Like Byron, he prefers to rattle on exactly as he'd talk to anybody on a ride or walk. Surrey also defended himself when on trial for his life some six years later with haughty and pungent scorn ; but the three poems which he then wrote preserve nothing of this. He had a cool, detached view of the art of poetry, and even when he knew that he must shortly die, he was less concerned with self-revelation than with the perfecting of a work of art.

> *The storms are past, these clouds are over-blown,*
> *And humble cheer great rigour hath repressed ;*
> *For the default is set a pain foreknown,*
> *And patience graft in a determined breast.*
> *And in the heart where heaps of griefs were grown*

The sweet revenge hath planted mirth and rest ;
No company so pleasant as mine own.

This was his last poem, his son said. Surrey could see himself from without, and rejoice in the sweet revenge which his calm defiance of his enemies had given him. Such aloofness is neither inhuman nor ignoble : it is a distinguishing mark of the finest artists, the quality which Coleridge detected in Shakespeare's early poems, and took to be the most sure sign of his coming greatness.

George Puttenham, writing his *Art of English Poetry* for the next generation, said that he could see little difference between the poetry of Surrey and Wyatt. This was not just critical insensibility. Puttenham, like other Elizabethans, was most interested in those poems where the new influences of the Italian Renaissance and of classicism were most apparent. So far as Wyatt was concerned therefore, he was thinking of his versions of Petrarch's sonnets, of *strambotti* by Serafino dell' Aquila, or of *rondeaux* by Marot. At such things Surrey was much more accomplished than Wyatt, but he hardly attempted the sort of poem for which we now most value Wyatt. The association of their two names, though inevitable because of their association in *Songs and Sonnets*, is thus misleading. They must be considered separately, for their own individual qualities, which are quite distinct.

Surrey cannot have had much opportunity of knowing Wyatt personally. He was fourteen years younger, closer in age to Wyatt's son, whom he did know, and, except when he went to France with the Duke of Richmond in 1532, when Wyatt also accompanied Henry VIII, they were seldom in the same place at the same time. But Surrey admired Wyatt as a poet, and on his death wrote an excellent elegy and two not very good sonnets. None of these records any personal feeling of loss. The elegy was in the stanza which Gray long afterwards used for his *Elegy*. They had in common a dislike of speaking out, though derived in Gray from diffidence, and in Surrey from an aristocratic disdain for raising his voice. The elegy was published shortly after Wyatt's death, and was Surrey's first published poem. So far as is known this poem, unlike the sonnet on Thomas Clere, was never inscribed on a tomb, though it may well have been painted on a board to be hung on Wyatt's hearse in the fashion of the time. (Its opening line,

Wyatt resteth here, that quick could never rest,

suggests that it was so intended.) It has Surrey's character-istic quality of classical restraint and brevity, and reads like an epitaph. It is altogether different from any previous funerary poem in English, but it has had many successors, most of them less distinguished.

Surrey comes nearest to Wyatt's manner in

London, hast thou accused me,

written when he and some friends, Wyatt's son among them, had been imprisoned for some rowdy youthful behaviour, breaking windows, alarming middle-aged citizens, and shooting pellets at Bankside tarts. There is an impromptu quality about the poem : it is for the most part in *terza rima*, but a dozen lines in the middle have not been brought into the pattern, and one line has two redundant syllables. Such carelessness was far from typical of Surrey, and in another poem he demonstrates that he could manage the difficulties of *terza rima* perfectly well when he wished. It seems likely then that the poem was dashed off in haste, in prison, and that Surrey never bothered to revise it : such personal out-bursts were not to his taste. Elsewhere Surrey occasionally echoes a phrase from a poem by Wyatt, but this indicates no more than that he knew them. He was not influenced by Wyatt, except in his use of Poulter's measure, which only shows how unfortunate such an influence can be. Even here, as C. S. Lewis pointed out, Surrey demonstrated his extraordinary technical mastery in making something out of this notoriously disastrous metre.

Again unlike Wyatt, Surrey probably never wrote a poem which he intended for singing. There are half a dozen or so poems in stanzas, but except perhaps for the gay and lively

Give place, ye lovers, here before,

these are not songs. One of these stanzaic poems,

O happy dames that may embrace,

is as moving as anything he ever wrote. But he does not write here from his own point of view : he puts the words, in the manner of Ovid's *Heroides*, into the mouth of his beloved Countess waiting in England while he is absent at the wars in France.

> *When other lovers in arms across*
> *Rejoice their chief delight,*
> *Drowned in tears to mourn my loss*
> *I stand the bitter night*
> *In my window, where I may see*
> *Before the winds how the clouds flee.*
> *Lo, what a mariner love hath made me !*

There is a reminiscence here of Dido standing by her window and seeing Aeneas depart with his fleet from Carthage, but touched in so lightly that Dido's grief alone, nothing of her vengeful anger, is conveyed. Surrey's stanza is original, and as always he gains a contrapuntal effect by varying the syntactical pattern against the metrical pattern, while the lengthening of the final line adds to the pathetic movement of the whole. The subtlety of this would be concealed by musical setting.

This poem was given a dramatic context. But a poem which he wrote when he was imprisoned at Windsor,

So cruel prison how could betide, alas !

is personal. It has something of Wyatt's vigour but also a polished felicity which Wyatt never achieved. Surrey contrasts his present plight with his former happiness at Windsor as the companion of the young Duke of Richmond, who had died the year before. Most poets, and certainly most youthful poets — Surrey was twenty at the time — would have mourned the loss : Surrey re-creates their old happiness at proud Windsor,

Where each sweet place returns a taste full sour,
The large green courts, where we were wont to hove,
With eyes cast up unto the maidens' tower,
And easy sighs, such as folk draw in love.

The stately sales ; the ladies bright of hue ;
The dances short ; long tales of great delight.
With words and looks that tigers could but rue,
Where each of us did plead the other's right.

The palm play where, despoiled for the game,
With dazed eyes oft we by gleams of love
Have missed the ball and got sight of our dame,
To bait her eyes which kept the leads above.

The gravelled ground, with sleeves tied on the helm,
On foaming horse, with swords and friendly hearts,
With cheer as though the one should overwhelm,
Where we have fought and chased oft with darts.

All the glitter and gallantry of their splendid youth is here, the formal compliment of *amour courtois* and its extravagance of language which would move even such unfeeling brutes as tigers ; the games and the tournament before a gallery of fair ladies ; the anxieties of love, and the excitement of stag hunting in the wild forest ; the intimacies of friendship,

> *The secret thoughts imparted with such trust,*
> *The wanton talk, the diverse change of play,*
> *The friendship sworn, each promise kept so just,*
> *Wherewith we passed the winter nights away.*

With masterly economy Surrey depicts the life at that Court which the King meant to rival those of other Renaissance princes, and of which he was the most brilliant ornament. For that society he wrote his poems, some of which are preserved in the manuscript where his sister, the Duchess of Richmond, and two of her friends, Margaret Douglas, the King's niece, and Mary Shelton, wrote down poems by Wyatt and others of their friends. Sir George Blage, whom Surrey addressed in one of the poems written during his last imprisonment, made another such collection which survives, with at least three of Surrey's poems in it along with more of Wyatt's. We may suppose that many another courtier copied into his commonplace book the poems which Surrey circulated, and of which many must surely have been lost.

Perhaps he had the same company in mind when he set out to translate the *Aeneid*. They enjoyed songs, and sonnets, but also (as he remarked) 'long tales of great delight', and if most of these were romances, yet might he not have hoped to win them to the more serious tales of the Fall of Troy, and of the love of Dido and Aeneas ? Or had he also, perhaps unrecognized, Spenser's motive, to show that modern English, no less than Chaucer's, could encompass stories of such magnitude ? Certainly that was his achievement, or one of his achievements, and since all societies that have much valued poetry have been ambitious to attempt poems on a grand scale, to rival Homer, or Virgil, or Ariosto, or Milton, it is no wonder that, until our own day, Surrey was preferred above any other poet of his time.

Revaluation of his poetry is overdue. He was an innovator, a forerunner, one who pointed the way to poets who had greater gifts, and more time ; the 'noble, valiant, eloquent Englishman' of Mr Blunden's sonnet,

> *Who led our language and our interest*
> *Up shining ways, which should all England school.*

But gratitude is not a critical virtue : we are to judge poets for what they did themselves not for what help or hindrance they left to their successors. The best of Surrey's poetry can give pleasure not only for the suggestion of greater things to come, but for itself ; not because he introduced the form of the sonnet and the blank verse to which Shakespeare gave such majesty, but because he used them with distinction ; not historic therefore but true poetic pleasure.

TEXT

Poems, ed. Emrys Jones, Oxford, Clarendon Press, 1964. See also Kenneth Muir in *Notes and Queries*, 1960, pp. 369–70.

3

GEORGE GASCOIGNE

GEORGE GASCOIGNE, the elder son of Sir John Gascoigne, M.P., of Cardington, Yorkshire, was, like Wyatt, an English country gentleman affected by the ambitions of a Renaissance courtier. In him the later Elizabethans recognized the most gifted poet among their immediate predecessors while at the same time they saw that he had failed, through some lack of concentration, to develop his gifts to their full excellence. Their judgment is just, but is worth examining, to discover again the promise of his poetry and the causes of its lack of fulfilment. For his poems are not in themselves disappointing, but a man who tried so many kinds, and who thought so lucidly about his art, ought not to have stopped short : when greatness was within his reach he allowed himself to be distracted.

He was born in the late 1530s, went up to Cambridge, probably to Trinity College, and in 1555 was admitted a member of Gray's Inn. He visited France and attended the French Court at the magnificent new palace of Fontainebleau, where he wrote two of his earliest poems, sonnets on the English model which Surrey had recently invented. He was back in England early in 1558 when he was elected to Queen Mary's last Parliament as member for Bedford, and in the autumn of the year he heard in Parliament the news of Queen Mary's death and the proclamation of Queen Elizabeth. The following January he attended her Coronation with the hereditary official duty of Almoner, and was for a time much at Court. So far his career had been convention-ally satisfactory : the son of a rich landowner in the North of England whose marriage had further increased the family property, he had acquired the fashionable polish during a visit to the French Court, had tried his hand at the new form of the sonnet, had been elected, like his father, to the House of Commons, and had attended the young Queen at her Coronation. He had not paid any serious attention to his legal studies preferring, as he said later, 'to catch a courtly grace'. And why not ? He was well-bred, handsome, and intelligent, and must have been conscious of an unusual talent ; he was rich ; he was young. Delighted by the prospect of serving a Queen who was only three or four years older than himself, he shared to the full the excitement of the new reign which the Queen's favourite device of the Phoenix reborn symbolized as a new golden age. As Gas-coigne himself recalled,

> The stately pomp of princes and their peers
> Did seem to swim in floods of beaten gold ;
> The wanton world of young delightful years
> Was not unlike a heaven to behold.

No wonder, then, that he was ambitious to cut a figure in this gay and splendid world. But like many another rich young man, he was inclined in his inexperience to over-estimate his wealth ; he was indiscreet, and contentious, and had a knack of getting into trouble ; and he soon found that charm did not invariably provide a way out.

A few days before the Coronation of Queen Elizabeth there died one William Breton, a prosperous citizen of London, leaving a widow and several young children, among them the poet Nicholas Breton. Elizabeth Breton, the widow, went through some form of marriage three months later, in April 1559, with a man named Edward Boyes. But George Gascoigne, who must have been eight or ten years younger than she, also sought her in marriage and on 23 November 1561, whether bigamously or not, did marry her. The intricacies of these marriages need not concern us, but they involved Gascoigne in much expensive litigation before he could get rid of Boyes, from whom eventually Elizabeth obtained a divorce; and a second marriage to Gascoigne took place. These matters continued for four or five years and if they suggest a romantic impulsiveness on the part of Gascoigne, they also suggest its normal associate, a lack of common sense.

In addition to these marital complications Gascoigne was finding life at Court more and more expensive, and he was soon selling property in order to keep going. Living on capital is seldom advisable in one's twenties, and this Gascoigne learnt (as he always had to learn) the hard way.

> *Of every farm I then let fly a lease*
> *To feed the purse that paid for peevishness,*
> *Till rent and all were fallen in such disease*
> *As scarce could serve to maintain cleanliness.*

To such a condition had five years spendthrift life at Court reduced him, and by the autumn of 1563 he and his wife (or Boyes's wife, or whoever's wife she was) were living in the country at Willington in Bedfordshire. A year or so later he decided to return to Gray's Inn, with the hope that a resumption of his legal studies might put him in the way to earning his living. Five of his fellow-students there proposed themes on which he was to write poems for them before being accepted back into their company.

George Gascoigne

These poems (so the editor in whose hands he left them when he went overseas tells us) Gascoigne composed 'riding by the way, writing none of them until he came at the end of his journey, the which was no longer than one day in riding, one day in tarrying with his friend, and the third in returning to Gray's Inn'. The casual brilliance of such a feat — the poems include eight sonnets, and others in rhyme royal, in cross-rhyme, and in rhymed alexandrines — is characteristic both for its virtuosity and for its casualness. The negligent ease of *sprezzatura* which every young man of the sixteenth century hoped to attain came naturally to the gifted, irresponsible Gascoigne. But it is probable that a poet who could write so well riding up to London from Bedfordshire could have written better still with a little more consideration. The poems have a witty, rueful candour as he looks back over his mis-spent youth. John Vaughan had proposed as his theme *Magnum vectigal parcimonia*, 'Thrift is a great income', with a humorous suggestion that his friend Gascoigne might try it, for a change. Gascoigne begins his lines, as Wyatt would have done, with a proverb :

> *The common speech is, Spend and God will send ;*
> *But what sends he ? — a bottle and a bag,*
> *A staff, a wallet, and a woeful end*
> *For such as list in bravery so to brag.*

Again, he develops Antony Kinwelmarsh's theme *Satis sufficit* in a series of variations in rhyme royal on the proverb 'Enough is as good as a feast'.

The best of these poems are the seven linked sonnets to Alexander Nevill on the theme *Sat cito, si sat bene*, which Gascoigne paraphrased as 'No haste but good'. In these he traces his reckless career at Court with his usual forthrightness, and without self-pity : he is well aware of his impatience to shine in the Court, and of his extravagant expenditure in trying to achieve his ambitions there.

> *To prink me up and make me higher placed,*
> *All came too late that tarried any time.*
> *Piles of provision pleased not my taste,*
> *They made my heels too heavy for to climb.*

But the inevitable result of his improvidence was that soon he could scarcely afford clean linen and he had to withdraw from Court to live quietly in the country.

These clear-sighted comments on his own folly are disarming, but it is doubtful whether the friends who set him these penitential themes believed in his coming reformation. Rather, knowing his gift for improvisation, they decided to tease him by setting moral themes for him to commend to himself in witty verse. Repentance for wasted youth was not to cut him off from their company, but to provide them with literary amusement. And when he was back with them at Gray's Inn his devotion to legal studies cannot have been very serious, for, responsive as always to the literary taste of his companions, he immediately set about translating two plays from the Italian, from Ariosto the play he called *Supposes*, and from Dolce *Giocasta*. This last was the first English version ever made of a Greek play, but its derivation from Euripides' *Phoenissae* is at third hand, through Latin and Italian. Both plays were acted in Gray's Inn in 1566.

Next year Gascoigne abandoned his pretence of studying the law, and went back to his father's estate in Yorkshire. Perhaps Sir John felt his health failing, and sent for his heir, for soon afterwards, in 1568, he died, and George came into a considerable inheritance. But the man who had so soon dissipated his wife's fortune found no more difficulty in wasting his patrimony, and by April 1570 he was in Bedford Gaol for debt. To such a state had the dashing young courtier of twelve years before come through feckless improvidence, and doubtful honesty. For, as his biographer sadly admits, 'all financial transactions in which Gascoigne was involved seem to have been questionable'.

How long he remained in prison we do not know, but there was nothing for it, on his release, but to try to restore his finances by serving as a soldier of fortune in the Low Countries. He sailed to Flushing in June 1572, and soon saw action ; but the expedition proved a failure, and by November he was back in England, sadder and wiser (it may be) but certainly no richer. Now at last he turned to his one true talent, for writing, in order to start on the slow climb back to prosperity. He had published nothing, but his elegant and witty poems had circulated among his friends at Court and among the lawyers, and had won some reputation. He was well connected, and so was his wife, a Bacon by birth. He had made enemies, but he still had friends, many of whom would be willing to help him, if only he would show some signs of conducting himself more responsibly. Soon after his return home Viscount Montague asked him to write a masque for the double wedding of his son and heir Anthony Browne to Mary Dormer and of his daughter Elizabeth to Robert Dormer, Mary's brother ; he was to provide them with an excuse for wearing Venetian costume. This Gascoigne achieved by connecting the Montagues of Cowdray with the Montagues of Italy — Romeo's family.* Then one of his neighbours in Bedfordshire, Lord Grey, to whom he had addressed a poem from Holland some months

* Anthony Browne had another sister, Mary, who married Henry Wriothesley, and became the mother of the Earl of Southampton to whom Shakespeare dedicated *Venus and Adonis* and *Lucrece*.

before, invited him to hunt the deer on his estates there.
Gascoigne was a poor shot, it seems, for 'shooting very often,
he could never hit any deer ; yea, and often times he let the
herd pass by as though he had not seen them'. Lord Grey
made some remark on this, and Gascoigne addressed a poem
to him, called *Gascoigne's Woodmanship* in which he recounted
the failures of his life, to show that failure to hit the deer was
nothing strange in him, for

He shoots awry almost at every mark.

Among these marks had been philosophy, law, courtly
grace, and lately soldiering,

Mistrusting all the virtues of the mind
He trusts the power of his personage,
As though long limbs led by a lusty heart
Might yet suffice to make him sick again.
But Flushing frays have taught him such a part
That now he thinks the wars yield no such gain.
And sure I fear, unless your lordship deign
To train him yet into some better trade,
It will be long before he hit the vein
Whereby he may a richer man be made.

Lord Grey, whom Spenser was later to serve in Ireland, was
already showing himself a patron of English poetry.

Encouraged by all this Gascoigne now began to collect
his poems together for publication, but before he had completed the task he returned precipitately to the wars in
Holland. There seems little doubt that the reason for this
was to avoid answering objections which had been sent to
the Privy Council against his admission to Parliament.
(Through Lord Montague's influence he had been returned,
at a by-election, for Midhurst.) The charges brought against

him were that he owed money 'to a great number of persons' (who would be denied redress through his Parliamentary immunity), that he was guilty of manslaughter, that he was a ruffian, a spy, an atheist, 'a common rhymer and a deviser of slanderous pasquils against divers persons of great calling'. It was not, after all, going to be so easy to live down his past, and Gascoigne, having got wind of these charges, decided to go back to the wars. He left on 19 March in the company of one Rowland Yorke, whom Camden describes as 'a man of a loose and dissolute behaviour, and desperately audacious, famous in his time amongst the common hacksters and swaggerers', the sort of man whose friendship might help the charge of 'ruffian' to stick. The lack of discretion which Gascoigne had noted in himself in his poem to Lord Grey had not yet been remedied.

This time Gascoigne remained in the Netherlands for eighteen months, again taking part in several actions, becoming more and more disillusioned by the lack of discipline and general incompetence. As we should expect he soon got into trouble through indiscretion. In July he had an affair with a Dutch lady at The Hague, and gave her his picture. Three months later the Spaniards captured The Hague, and the lady sent her maid to Gascoigne, now with the Prince of Orange, whom he greatly admired, at Delft. The girl was stopped and questioned, and the Dutch naturally suspected that Gascoigne was plotting to hand over the town to the enemy. Gascoigne for once acted sensibly, and showed the letter to the Prince, who accepted his explanation ; but some suspicion remained in the minds of others. Gascoigne stayed on and in the spring took command of a company of volunteers, but as usual his luck was out and early in the summer he was taken prisoner outside the walls of Leiden. He was well enough treated and after the campaigning season was over he was released, and returned to England in October 1574.

During his absence his first book *A Hundreth Sundrie Flowres* had been published and (it seems scarcely necessary to say) had brought still more trouble upon him. Some of the poems, as he puts it, had 'been doubtfully construed, and therefore scandalous'. These were mostly early poems from his days at Court, and the subjects of some of them resented his references; also, the short novel printed in the same volume, *The Adventures of Master F. J.* was being interpreted as a *roman à clef*. The old charge that he was 'a deviser of slanderous pasquils' had not been forgotten. He therefore put out, in the year after his return, a new edition of his book now called *The Posies of George Gascoigne*, in which he re-arranged, or rather disarranged, the order of the poems in order to conceal the identity of the persons to whom they referred, and a few he omitted altogether. In 1573 he had suggested that the initials F. J. might be expanded to 'Freeman Jones'. Now in 1575 he proposed 'Ferdinando Jeronimi', and ascribed the work to a non-existent Italian author, Bartello. It seems a bit thin, but apparently it sufficed.

However for us, who are not much shocked by Court gossip of the 1560s, it is better to read the poems in their original, more or less chronological, order. But first we should consider the short essay, *Certayne Notes of Instruction concerning the making of verse or ryme in English*, which Gascoigne added in 1575, and which is the first piece of critical writing by an English poet.

'The first and most necessary point' (he begins) 'that ever I found meet to be considered in making of a delectable poem is this, to ground it upon some fine invention.' By invention he means that imaginative element in a poem which differentiates it from the literal and factual. Gascoigne, like all the poets of his own age and the succeeding age, always had his mind on the finished poem as a work of art. Their concern was not the Romantic concern with self-expression (though few have written more candidly about themselves than Gascoigne) but with making a good sonnet, or a good song, or a good pastoral. They kept in mind the audience for whom they wrote — a mistress, a learned and witty friend, a visitor reading an epitaph on a tomb, 'a gentleman or noble person', the groundlings in the Globe Theatre. (Sir Philip Sidney in the first sonnet of *Astrophel and Stella* declares that he has been 'studying inventions fine, her wits to entertain'.) Thus Gascoigne at once announces the critical principle on which all pre-Romantic poetry was founded. Ronsard, a few years before, had said the same : 'le principal poinct est l'invention'. Gabriel Harvey, in his copy of Gascoigne's book, noted against this passage, 'pregnant and notable points', and his friend Spenser would have agreed. So would Shakespeare, Jonson, Donne, Milton, Dryden, and Pope. Gascoigne goes on to advise in favour of clarity, of metrical consistency, of respect for the natural stress on words. He opposes the use of long, polysyllabic 'inkhorn' words. He gives sound advice on rhyme and on the use of rhetorical figures ; on discretion in the use of unusual words ; on avoidance of inversion. He describes various stanza forms, and recommends brevity. All is direct, practical, to the point. And the reader wonders why a man of such intelligence did not either keep to the sphere in which his mind worked so well or carry over these qualities into the conduct of his life.

Thus, though Gascoigne was a courtier poet, like Wyatt and Surrey, or like Sidney and Ralegh and Carew, he was also one who had thought seriously about the art of poetry.

He defends himself, in a preface to *The Posies*, for publishing his poems, and quotes the example of the Calvinist theologian Beza 'whose life is worthily become a lantern to the whole world, but who did not yet disdain to suffer the continued publication of such poems as he wrote in youth'. And he adds that patriotic motive which so much influenced the coming splendour of English poetry, and which Sidney and Mulcaster and many another would soon reaffirm : 'I have always been of opinion' (he says) 'that it is not unpossible either in poems or in prose to write both compendiously and perfectly in our English tongue'. It was by no means the universal opinion at that time.

There is good reason to believe that the arrangement of the poems in *A Hundreth Sundrie Flowres* is chronological. They are divided into eight groups, each denoted by a 'posy', a Latin motto, chosen by Gascoigne in the manner then in fashion, to indicate his mood at the time of writing. The first group contains among its twenty-one poems six sonnets, all in Surrey's new English form, and therefore probably to be dated after the publication of those poems in 1557. (The eighth poem refers to Gascoigne's contest for a wife with Boyes, and since it suggests that Boyes was successful at the time, it was presumably written in 1559 or 1560.) Gascoigne follows Surrey also in using the sonnet for other than the compliments of love ; and again like Surrey he puts poems into the mouth of a woman. These early poems have a courtly polish and are sometimes overladen with classical reference ; but most are appropriated by time and place, and are very personal. Usually Gascoigne heads his poems with a note on the occasion of their composition rather than with a title : 'He wrote unto a Scottish dame whom he chose for his mistress at the French Court, as followeth' ; 'He wrote (at his friend's request) in praise of a gentlewoman, whose name was Phillip, as followeth'. This is a gay and lively lyric:

> Of all the birds that I do know,
> Phillip my sparrow hath no peer :
> For sit she high, or lie she low,
> Be she far off, or be she near,
> There is no bird so fair, so fine,
> Nor yet so fresh as this of mine.

For though the fashionable love-melancholy of the courtly lover, and the convention of cruel lady and lovelorn youth, run through many of these poems, they are not unrelieved by high spirits. A sonnet is addressed 'To a Dame which challenged the author because he held his head always down and looked not upon her in his wonted wise'. He explained why this is so.

> The mouse which once hath broken out of trap
> Is seldom 'ticed with the trustless bait,
> But lieth aloof, for fear of more mishap.

This directness of expression comes out most clearly in some of the lyrics, in which Gascoigne, like Wyatt, follows the natural English order of words, as he recommends in the *Notes of Instruction*. 'The lover disdainfully rejected contrary to former promise, thus complaineth' :

> The deadly drops of dark disdain
> Which daily fall on my desart ;
> The lingering suit long spent in vain,
> Whereof I feel no fruit but smart ;
> Enforce me now these words to write,
> Not all for love, but more for spite.

The which to thee I must rehearse,
Whom I did honour, serve, and trust.
And though the music of my verse
Be plainsong tune both true and just,
Content thee yet to hear my song,
For else thou dost me double wrong.

Again like Wyatt he is fond of using proverbs, though he does not use them so much as Wyatt, and would never have claimed to prefer 'the common sort' to the courtiers. Indeed, after quoting some proverbs on one occasion he renounces them :

I compt him but a beast
Which trusteth truth to dwell in common speech.

And he differs from Wyatt in preferring to break up the stanza (as in those just quoted) into short sentences, which denies him the subtler effects which Wyatt sometimes achieved. But in this Gascoigne was reacting against ink-horn terms and aureation, and he associated complex sentence structure with the use of long words, which he abhorred. His preference for simplicity and brevity was, at that time, very commendable, and he succeeds best in the lyrics which this manner especially suits. The best known of all these is probably the poem entitled *Gascoigne's Lullaby.*

Sing lullaby, as women do,
Wherewith they bring their babes to rest,
And lullaby can I sing too
As womanly as can the best.
With lullaby they still the child,
And if I be not much beguiled,
Full many wanton babes have I
Which must be stilled with lullaby.

These wanton babes, as he lists them, are his 'youthful years', his 'gazing eyes', his 'wanton will' and so on. Out of the *berceuse* form he makes an ironical poem of farewell to youth, which ends :

> *Thus lullaby my youth, mine eyes,*
> *My will, my ware, and all that was.*
> *I can no more delays devise ;*
> *But welcome pain, let pleasure pass.*
> *With lullaby now take your leave,*
> *With lullaby your dreams deceive ;*
> *And when you rise with waking eye,*
> *Remember Gascoigne's Lullaby.*

This, like many another of his poems, including a few pious pieces, was set to music.

Signs of eventual reformation appear both in these divine poems and in the latest poems in the book, written after he left for Holland in the early summer of 1572, which include an epitaph on an English captain, Bourcher, who was killed in the wars there. But Gascoigne summed up his views on war in a poem first published in *The Posies*, which he called *The Fruites of Warre*, and for which he took the theme *Dulce Bellum Inexpertis*. This poem which runs to over fourteen hundred lines in rhyme royal, was 'written by piecemeal at sundry times, as the author had vacant leisure from service, being begun at Delft in Holland'. He refers the reader to a lengthy discourse on the same theme by Erasmus in the *Adagia*. So once again he confirms that he 'wanted not learning', at the same time as he writes while subject to more than his usual distraction. The poem is the first of its kind, and is written from a highly individual point of view ; the first war poem in modern English written by a man who had taken part in war, and who, when he wrote it, was liable to all the interruptions of active service.

He begins, in the traditional way, from authority, but he rejects the descriptions of war by poets, painters, and the common voice, and, in a phrase which Marlowe remembered, he substitutes his own view of war :

I say that war is even the scourge of God.

He follows with stanzas of warning against war addressed to 'the wiser sort' in society, Prince, Nobility, Prelacy, even Lawyers, Merchants, and Husbandmen, of which the general purport is 'Be content with what you have'. He dismisses the pursuit of honour and the hope of riches as alike futile ; and he lists various reasons why men try their luck in wars, with a characteristic, ironical glance at himself. Men have fled from Court, he says,

> *Some for their own speech, some for other men's,*
> *Some for their books, because they wrote too much,*
> *Yea, some for rhymes, — but sure I know none such.*

This long general preamble on the evils of war, more than one third of the whole poem, is followed by an account of personal experiences, which, to modern taste, is the more valuable part of the poem, though the earlier part is not dull. (Gascoigne is never that.) In this we have Gascoigne's usual disarming candour : he tells of the scrape he got into when his mistress's letter was intercepted at Delft, he describes the mismanaged, unheroic operations in which he took part ; his interviews with William of Orange ; his difficulties with underfed and mutinous troops, and unhelpful allies ; finally he tells of their surrender upon terms, honourable imprisonment, and release. Here is no pacifist tirade against war, no romantic assertion that the poetry of war is in the pity, but instead the dry self-deprecating humour of a man of action who sees, above all, the folly of war and the degradation which it brings. This was the typical Elizabethan attitude to war, from the Queen herself down : war, to them, was an uncivilized pursuit appropriate to the middle ages, not to their own times, and they were disposed to laugh at avoidable heroics, though, like any other men, they would admire courage. Gascoigne ends his poem with praise of the Queen

> *whose high foresight provides*
> *That waste of war your realms doth not destroy.*

That, too, was a favourite theme with Elizabethan poets. Gascoigne's poem is very much a soldier's poem. As such it shocked civilians like Gabriel Harvey, who noted that it was 'a good pragmatic discourse, but unseasonable, and most unfit for a captain, or professed martialist'. Then, as now, it was the man who stays safely at home in an academic or civil service post who most fervently requires demonstrations of fire-eating.

From the time of his return to England from military service, two years before, Gascoigne had been a reformed character. Even at Court his reformation was seen to be genuine, in spite of all the evidence to its improbability which his old acquaintance there would hardly wish to be so soon forgotten. He had published prose works with such resounding titles as *The Droomme of Doomes day*, and *A delicate Diet, for daintiemouthde Droonkards*. He had been commissioned by Leicester to provide a suitable entertainment for the Queen on her famous visit to Kenilworth in July 1575, and later in the same summer he wrote *The Tale of Hemetes the Heremyte* to be performed in her presence at Woodstock. Of this, on New Year's Day 1576, he presented her with an elaborate manuscript copy, in the front of which is a picture of the poet kneeling before the Queen in the act of handing her his book. The drawing which shows the Queen enthroned and Gascoigne with a laurel wreath above his head, is by Gascoigne himself and so are the translations of the *Tale* into Latin, Italian, and French. On a scroll is Gascoigne's favourite motto *Tam Marti quam Mercurio*, later to be used of Sir Philip Sidney, to indicate that he partook of the life of action and of the life of the mind, in accordance with the ideals of the Renaissance courtiers. In token of this Gascoigne, portrayed in civilian dress, holds a spear in his left hand, and in his poetic address to the Queen, after explaining the symbolism, he begs his 'peerless prince' to

> *employ this willing man*
> *In your affairs to do the best he can.*

His appeal was answered, for later in the year he was sent back to the Low Countries as an observer on behalf of the English Government. In the autumn he found himself in the thick of the fighting at Antwerp. The city fell on 4 November ; Gascoigne got away on the 12th, was back in England by the 21st, wrote his account *The Spoyle of Antwerpe* on the 25th, and had it in print by the end of the month. This vivid piece of journalism, a war correspondent's account of the siege and sack of the city, is also without parallel in the sixteenth century.

In April, before leaving for the Continent, Gascoigne had dedicated to Lord Grey two more poems, *The Complaynt of Philomene* which had been begun before in April 1562, and a satire *The Steele Glas*. Gascoigne seems to have been often prompted to poetry while on horseback, for he began *The*

Complaynt, he says, 'riding by the high way between Chelms-
ford and London', and his reason for not then finishing it is
no less characteristic of him : 'being overtaken by a sudden
dash of rain, I changed my copy . . . leaving *The Complaynt of
Philomene* unfinished'. On that journey, he said, 'his mind
mused upon the days passed, and therewithal he gan accuse
his own conscience of much time mis-spent'. The weather
had looked fine when he set out, and he was without his
cloak, so the sudden shower gave him further cause 'to
accuse himself of his carelessness'. This prompted a sonnet,
and afterwards the *De Profundis*. He took up the *Complaynt*
again in April 1575, and finally completed it a year later. In
conception therefore it properly belongs with the short
poems of *An Hundreth Sundrie Flowres*, but the reformed
Gascoigne of these later days makes the retelling of the classical myth of Tereus, Progne, and Philomela morally didactic.
It is a warning against lust and the injury thereby inflicted on
the innocent, and it concludes with a demonstration of the
inexorable punishment of wickedness and vice. This savage
tale which Ovid tells in the sixth book of the *Metamorphoses*
had already been recounted in English by Chaucer in *The
Legend of Good Women*, and by Gower in *Confessio Amantis*.
No doubt Gascoigne knew these versions, but he certainly
used Ovid also. Not until 1589, when Lodge published his
Scillaes Metamorphosis did any English poet break with the
mediaeval tradition of *Ovide moralisé*, and the Poulter's measure
in which *The Complaynt* is written emphasizes the backward
looking nature of the poem. In all Gascoigne's work it is
the only poem of which this can be said ; that provi-
dential shower of rain in 1562 ought not to have been
disregarded.

With this poem Gascoigne published *The Steele Glas*, as if
to contrast with the old-fashioned manner of *The Complaynt*

the modernity of his satire, which is the first original English poem in blank verse. (This again suggests the influence of Surrey, the most forward-looking of Gascoigne's recent predecessors.) The poem is, at the beginning, linked to *The Complaynt* by a rather dubious analogy which Gascoigne draws between himself and the innocent victim of Tereus, whose tongue had been cut out, just as (he suggests) his poems had been suppressed. However, this is too far-fetched for Gascoigne to continue for long, and he soon comes to his main satire, on the corruptions of the age which have been brought about by new social fashions, and the rise of new men. The satire gains force from the fact that Gascoigne, in his youth, had been a fashionable courtier. 'I have mis-governed my youth,' he says in his dedication to Lord Grey, 'I confess it . . . I am rigorously rejected when I proffer amends for my harm.' It is impossible to regain a reputation, how-ever sincere the repentance, because the characteristic vices of the age are envy and detraction, and because the fierce competition of the time allows no recovery. Perhaps his following of *Piers Plowman* rather than Wyatt and Alamanni in his satire is significant of his rejection of the courtly Italian fashions of his earlier poetry. But however conservative his social attitude, in *The Steele Glas* Gascoigne, as always, dis-closes his own strong, original, independent quality, most notably in his use of the new blank verse.

His lines, like Marlowe's, or Shakespeare's at first, tend to be end-stopped, and not to achieve the rhythmical variety of Surrey's *Aeneid*. But Gascoigne always had a good ear, and he eschews alliteration now much more than in his earlier rhymed verse. Blank verse, by its very nature, is not alto-gether suitable for satire : it lacks the sharp point that can so well be given in heroic couplet or *ottava rima*. Sometimes Gascoigne attempts the antithetical effect which gives so much character to Augustan satire, enabling Dryden or Pope constantly to contrast the world as it is and the world as it might be ; but in so loose a form as blank verse these antitheses tend to become entries in a catalogue.

On New Year's Day 1577 Gascoigne presented to the Queen, to whom also he dedicated it, his last work *The Grief of Joye*, four poems in rhyme royal on the vanity of human life. He had written the poems while on the Continent in the Queen's service the previous summer, and the fourth of them breaks off in an unfinished stanza, with this note added : 'Left unperfect for fear of horsemen'. Those horsemen no doubt were the same to which he refers in *The Spoyle of Antwerpe* : 'On Sunday, the fourth of this instant in the morning, they all met at the said Castle. And their powers (as far as I could gather) were these : there came from Maastricht very near to a thousand horsemen, led by Don Alonso de Vergas.' This was the day, 4 November 1576, on which Antwerp fell. For these poems he returned to a Petrarchan model — not to the sonnets which had been part of the inspiration of his early love poems, but to Petrarch's Latin prose dialogue, *De Remediis utriusque Fortunae*. By an odd chance Catherine of Aragon had once invited Sir Thomas Wyatt to translate this for her. Wyatt began the task but abandoned it, he said, because 'after I had made proof of nine or ten dialogues, the labour began to seem tedious'. Now, exactly half a century later, George Gascoigne offered his poems to Queen Elizabeth. They are not in any sense translations or paraphrases of Petrarch's work, but, as Gascoigne acknowledges, they do derive from it. As always with Gascoigne, there is a strongly personal point of view, in his lament for the passing of youth and beauty and strength. For this reason the poems come alive, and are not vague moral generalizations.

There is a grief in every kind of joy,
That is my theme, and that I mean to prove.

In the second poem, which is entitled *The Vanities of Beauty*, Gascoigne gives the work a local habitation in Queen Elizabeth's Court, and a series of names, of ladies who are identified (and are still identifiable) by their initials in the margin, and who come to refute the charge brought by his Muse. Gascoigne gives a lively picture of infatuated Elizabethan lovers :

> *They set their ruffs, they ruffle up their hair,*
> *They talk far off, — their minds are otherwhere.*
> *They course the glass and let it take no rest.*
> *They peep and spy who gazeth on their face.*
> *They darkly ask whose beauty seemeth best.*
> *They hark and mark who marketh most their grace.*
> *They stay their steps and stalk a stately pace.*
> *They jealous are of every sight they see.*
> *They strive to seem, but never care to be.*

And so on ; a whole catalogue of youthful affectations such as Hilliard had already begun to record in his exquisite miniatures, such as Spenser would soon laugh at in *Colin Clouts Come Home Againe*. But in Gascoigne's poem we are aware that all the time he is looking back, in his detached, ironical way, at his own youth and the companions of it.

After this presentation to the Queen no more is known of Gascoigne's life. Probably he was in poor health — he had complained of this in the spring of 1576 — and on 7 October 1577 he died, at much the same age as Sir Thomas Wyatt. He was a man of genius, certainly, reflective (so far as concerned the art of poetry), energetic, quickly responsive to his surroundings, and able to write well in whatever fashion he there found. So he wrote Italianate sonnets and *novella* at Court, classical plays at Gray's Inn, a prodigal son play on the Dutch model after serving in Holland, war journalism in verse or prose while he was there, a masque for a society wedding, an entertainment for the Queen. Through it all he preserved his own vigorous, reckless, attractive identity, trusting the power of his personage (as he put it) rather than the powers of his mind. He learnt to see himself as others saw him, and to smile ironically at what he saw. But also he leaves the impression of a man who never gave himself time to develop his powers as an artist : we see him stuffing the unfinished sheets of a poem into his pockets when it comes on to rain, and forgetting them for twelve years ; thrusting another poem aside when the enemy cavalry burst in, and not, this time, taking it up again ; leaving a book of poems incomplete when he had to hurry off to the wars to evade his creditors.

Within two years of his death the anonymous commentator on Spenser's *The Shepheardes Calendar* said of Gascoigne that 'gifts of wit and natural promptness appear in him abundantly'. A few years later Nashe would acknowledge that Gascoigne 'first beat the path to that perfection which our best poets have aspired to since his departure'. Of these Spenser himself was the first, the herald of the New Poetry of the 1580s and 1590s. Gascoigne's poems were reprinted in 1587, but he was soon overshadowed by men of finer gifts who were more dedicated than he to the art of poetry. Michael Drayton, writing forty years after Gascoigne's death, said truly enough that had he and his contemporary, Churchyard,

> *Lived but a little longer, they had seen*
> *Their works before them to have buried been.*

57

Yet Gascoigne can still give something that no other poet gives — the wry, amused observation of a courtier, soldier, and scholar who, however feckless and disappointing in each role, at least kept a certain engaging candour, an unwillingness to be deceived even by himself. And that, surely, deserves our attention.

TEXTS

Works, ed. J. W. Cunliffe, 2 vols., Cambridge University Press, 1907, 1910.
A Hundreth Sundrie Flowres, ed. C. T. Prouty, New York, Columbia University Press, 1942.

4

MICHAEL DRAYTON

MICHAEL DRAYTON never had any other ambition than to be a poet. Throughout his life, from the time when, still a little boy, he entered as a page into the service of Sir Henry Goodere, the squire of a neighbouring village, to the evening before his death sixty years later, when he addressed his last poem to Sir Henry's daughter, he devoted all his intense energies to the fulfilment of that ambition. The son of a tanner in the Warwickshire village of Hartshill was not diverted from his true vocation by the social duties which distracted his betters, and he never had to face the dilemma which Francis Bacon so clearly recognized : 'Knowing myself by inward calling to be fitter to hold a book than to play a part, I have led my life in civil causes, for which I was not very fit by nature, and more unfit by the preoccupation of my mind'. Fascinated as Drayton was by the history of England, he had no wish to play an active part in the affairs of his own time, like Spenser or Milton ; and the Renaissance ideal of the active life he understood and admired and delighted to record but never chose to share.

He was born in 1563 a few months before Shakespeare, and a few miles from Stratford-upon-Avon. Their schoolboy years were not finished when the New Poetry was announced by the publication of *The Shepheardes Calendar*, but even before that Michael Drayton had felt the excitement with which poets were beginning to explore this copious new

English of his day. So, looking back in his fifties to those first beginnings of ambition, he told his friend Henry Reynolds (who had some small reputation as poet and critic) about them :

> *For from my cradle (you must know that) I*
> *Was still inclined to noble poesy,*
> *And when that once Pueriles I had read,*
> *And newly had my Cato construed,*
> *In my small self I greatly marvelled then,*
> *Amongst all other, what strange kind of men*
> *These poets were ; and, pleased with the name,*
> *To my mild tutor merrily I came,*
> *(For I was then a proper goodly page,*
> *Much like a pigmy, scarce ten years of age,)*
> *Clasping my slender arms about his thigh.*
> *'O my dear master ! cannot you,' (quoth I,)*
> *'Make me a poet ? do it, if you can,*
> *And you shall see, I'll quickly be a man.'*

The first poems which his kindly master read to him were the eclogues of Mantuan — 'good old Mantuan' of Shakespeare's recollection — and of Virgil, from whose classic grace and ease he quickly learnt to despise the popular ballads of the time. Thus was his taste for poetry first cultivated. Among English writers he would soon discover Wyatt and Surrey in the favourite anthology of the time *Songs and Sonnets* (which also Shakespeare remembered with pleasure) and the still living Gascoigne and Churchyard who

> *Accounted were great meterers many a day.*

We can imagine him picking up the latest volumes of poetry at Sir Henry Goodere's when his services as a page were for an hour not needed, and finding encouragement from his kind and well-read employer. To that 'happy and generous family' (Drayton gladly confessed) he owed the most part of his education. Sir Henry himself tried his hand, as a courtier should, at writing verses, was related in some degree of cousinship to Sir Philip Sidney, fought by his side at Zutphen, and was with him when he died a fortnight later at Arnhem. He was intimate enough with Sidney to be entrusted by him as he lay dying with the duty of carrying a jewel to the Queen 'as a remembrance of my most loyal and bounden duty to her Majesty'. Sidney's example as a patron of poets inspired 'many gentlemen excellently learned . . . to row and steer their course in his wake', and we may be sure that Sir Henry Goodere would have been proud to count himself among their number. When he died in 1595 he 'bequeathed' — it is Drayton's own word — he bequeathed his poet Michael Drayton to Lucy Countess of Bedford, no doubt because he foresaw the encouraging interest which she in her turn would find in poets and poetry.

Drayton was thus fortunate in being taken so early in life into a household where his childish ambition to be a poet would not be laughed at, or dismissed as absurd in a village lad, but given every chance to develop. Yet there was no suggestion of forcing a talent which was by no means precocious, and Drayton was twenty-eight before his first book *The Harmonie of the Church* was published. It consists of nineteen Biblical paraphrases, and if Sir Henry could see in these any promise that his former page would become a famous poet, he must have been a clairvoyant.

This was a false start, but thereafter Drayton began to respond to the taste of the age with a prompt sensitivity which never left him. He was not, like Spenser, a daring innovator and pioneer, but he was very quick to follow a lead and then to develop whatever kind it was — pastoral, sonnet, historical poem, ode, elegy — in a variety of ways, and with concentrated energy, until he had brought it to the best of which he was capable. For him, as for all his contemporaries, the art of poetry was a learned art, and he was always seeking the form most suited to his individual gifts ; if the perfection he hoped for eluded him until the kind was fashionable no longer, this did not trouble him, but he would continue to seek it in a world of pure imagination.

Nowhere is this more apparent than in his pastorals. The first of these was published in 1593, his second book, under the title of *Idea the Shepheards Garland*, and the last, *The Muses Elizium*, in 1630, his last book, the year before he died. Thus the writing of pastorals covered almost the whole of his working life, for he published others in 1606, 1619, and 1627. Virgil, to men of the Renaissance the arch-poet of all ages, had begun his public career as a poet with eclogues in the tradition of Theocritus, and Spenser had followed this recommended example with *The Shepheardes Calendar*. Drayton greatly admired these poems — Spenser, he said, 'had done enough for the immortality of his name, had he only given us his *Shepheardes Calendar*' — and in these first pastoral poems of 1593 he is a follower of the English Virgil. In so far as he ventures into experiments with rustic or archaic diction he plants his feet in Spenser's footsteps ; and as yet he shows little metrical invention. His landscape is realistic rather than ideal, but its inhabitants are not, like Spenser's shepherds, to be identified among contemporary Englishmen, for he lacked Spenser's characteristic boldness in using pastoral to discourse on matters of public controversy. He is at his best in his ballad of Dowsabell in the eighth eclogue, where he attempts something in the manner of the rhymed mediaeval romance which Chaucer's *Sir Thopas* parodied.

Far in the country of Arden
There wond a knight hight Cassemen
as bold as Isenbras :
Fell was he and eager bent,
In battle and in tournament
as was the good Sir Thopas.

The scene is set in Warwickshire's Arden ; Dowsabell's fresh beauty is compared to Derbyshire grass and Leominster wool ; the knight is as bold as Isenbras and (by suggestion) as bold as brass. There is a detached gaiety about the poem which promises well, and when Drayton revised these poems for his *Poems Lyrick and Pastoral*, 1606, he left this ballad almost untouched. This is all the more noticeable because elsewhere he removed most of the archaisms, and because it is the songs, rather than the dialogue or narrative parts, that he often revises most drastically or even rewrites.

In this poem we see him responding to the newer pastoral mode of the 1590s which *England's Helicon* so well illustrates. To that famous anthology Drayton contributed four songs, one which had already appeared in *The Shepheards Garland* but three of them new, which were to find their place in the eclogues of 1606. His language is more direct and precise, more in keeping with Sidney's precept,

A shepherd's tale no height of style requires,

approximating therefore to the classical plain style. Already in 1593 he had paid tribute to Sidney, but now, when even a few years of the new century had made that golden age of English poetry over whose beginnings Sidney had presided seem already remote, he replaced the earlier dirge with a longer and more heart-felt lament.

By 1619 Drayton felt confident enough in his pastorals to claim that they were ' bold upon a new strain, and must speak

for themselves'. What was this new strain? Spenser, whom
he praised in this same preface, was still his master, but
Drayton's pastoral landscape is never Arcadian but always
English, never an imaginary Mediterranean scene where (it
was supposed) the luscious clusters of the vine upon our
mouths do crush their wine, but the countryside of England
which Drayton, like Shakespeare, knew and loved so well.
Shakespeare's pastoral descriptions — the scene setting of
Venus and Adonis, the Forest of Arden, the sheep-shearing
scene in *A Winter's Tale* — are vivid, naturalistic records of
something he knew intimately from childhood. Drayton's
pastorals are like that too. We are not told of Parnassus,
Mount Ida, or Helicon, but of Meon Hill in Gloucestershire,
of Charnwood, of Hayles Abbey. As he says in one of his
sonnets

Fair Arden, thou my Tempe art alone,
And thou, sweet Anker, art my Helicon.

Drayton's shepherds have English names, and drink not
Hippocrene but cider ; they eat cheese and clotted cream and
sillabubs ; they dance morris dances to the sound of bag-
pipes ; and their dogs have names such as Whitefoot and
Cut-tail. The flowers too are as English as the flowers Per-
dita gathers ; and the birds are nightingales (of course) but
blackbirds, thrushes, and robins as well. All is done with
love, and is altogether delightful.

In these *Pastorals* of 1619 Drayton was still revising and
perfecting the poems which he had written as a young man,
a quarter of a century before. His friend William Browne of
Tavistock was writing his long, rambling poems, full of
Keatsian detail of observation, about this same time, but such
concern with the English countryside, whether of Warwickshire or Devon, was by now, in the heyday of the urban and

sophisticated wit of Donne and Carew and the rest, becoming a little outmoded.

One poem which Drayton wrote about 1613 or 1614,
The Shepheards Sirena, has some uncertain connection with
poems by William Browne and George Wither (another of
Drayton's friends). It consists of a long lyric with a refrain,
framed in narrative – the song, Drayton says, was written
first, and the narrative seems to have been intended to provide a fictitious setting for a poem which was probably, for
those in the know, otherwise based. The song has a metrical
gaiety which is irresistible.

> *Near to the silver Trent*
> *Sirena dwelleth :*
> *She to whom Nature lent*
> *all that excelleth :*
> *By which the Muses late,*
> *and the neat Graces,*
> *Have for their greater state*
> *taken their places :*
> *Twisting an anadem*
> *wherewith to crown her,*
> *As it belonged to them*
> *most to renown her.*
> Chorus.　*On thy bank*
> *In a rank*
> *Let thy swans sing her,*
> *And with their music*
> *along let them bring her.*

It is characteristic of Drayton, while concealing the identity
of Sirena, to be candid and particular about the countryside
where she lived – near to the Trent – and later in the poem we
hear of Dove and Derwent, of Moorland and Peak. These

clues indeed suggest that Sirena may have been Mary Curzon who lived at Croxall until her marriage in 1612 to Sir Edward Sackville. But in Drayton's poem she is less important than the scenery.

This poem, in spite of its English setting, is closer to the pastoral poetry which Drayton wrote in his sixties. Then undoubtedly he devised a new strain for pastoral. They have a cool, fresh delicacy about them far removed from the earthy, or earthly ; they are not concerned with the passion or perturbation of love — indeed the Queen of Love herself is banished in one of them, and an epithalamion in another is for a fairies' wedding. The shepherds and shepherdesses now have classical names such as Sirena and Dorilus and Cynthia instead of English ones, not because they are imagined inhabiting a Mediterranean Arcady but because they inhabit the *Muses' Elizium*, a world which looks back to the golden age of Elizabeth, as well as forward to the Elysium which the Muses contrive for their faithful poets. If these poems remind us of any other, it must be of Shakespeare's last plays, most of all of *The Tempest*, though I think Drayton reached this detached serenity independently, the culmination of a life devoted to the service of the Muses.

The Quest of Cynthia, like *The Shepheards Sirena*, was published in 1627, but has no local habitation in the English countryside, and no implied personal reference. Cynthia is certainly no mortal : she has the power so to enchant the water in which she bathes that it can (like Medea)

> *make one twenty in an hour*
> *Of Aeson's age before,*

something that the ageing poet must have longed for, and knew he might find in the secluded world of poetry. These airy quatrains are a sort of prelude to the nimphals — as

Drayton calls the Eclogues of *The Muses Elizium* — where the quest for Cynthia is finally achieved ; and surely it is no chance that the punning name *Elizium* occurs in the earlier poem. It is as if Drayton had all his life been seeking for this pure lyric poetry, aloof from worldly cares or personal ambition, and now in calm of mind he had found it.

> *A Paradise on earth is found,*
> *Though far from vulgar sight,*
> *Which with those pleasures doth abound*
> *That it Elizium hight.*
>
> *Where, in delights that never fade,*
> *The Muses lulled be,*
> *And sit at pleasure in the shade*
> *Of many a stately tree,*
>
> *Which no rough tempest makes to reel*
> *Nor their straight bodies bows ;*
> *Their lofty tops do never feel*
> *The weight of winter's snows.*

It is a land of perpetual spring, free from the sorrows of time passing — a golden world where the privileged may fleet their time carelessly.

> *The poet's Paradise this is,*
> *To which but few can come ;*
> *The Muses' only Bower of Bliss,*
> *Their dear Elizium.*

But it is an innocent Bower of Bliss, where happy souls may

> *spend the hours*
> *In harmless mirth and sport ;*

and which no Sir Guyon must destroy in the name of Temperance. Even the traditional song contests in which the nymphs engage imply no hostile rivalry, but are contests in the paying of compliments to each other. And when Cupid is presented, it is in the words of an ignorant ferryman who had transported him in his wherry :

> *I never saw the like, thought I.*
> *'Tis more than strange to me,*
> *To have a child have wings to fly,*
> *And yet want eyes to see.*

We hear in his speech the accents of a Thames waterman ; thus Drayton, like Shakespeare, or Herrick, by his humour and irony avoids the danger of mere prettiness which besets poetry of this kind.

The knowledge of a lifetime's observation of country crafts and of the English scene were not discarded. Forester and fisherman, no less than shepherds, disclose their expert knowledge and describe their way of life in an appeal to the nymphs, who cannot choose between them. A Coleridgean description of weather is English, not Italian :

> *Clear had the day been from the dawn,*
> *All chequered was the sky,*
> *Thin clouds like scarves of cobweb lawn*
> *Veiled heaven's most glorious eye.*
> *The wind had no more strength than this —*
> *That leisurely it blew,*
> *To make one leaf the next to kiss*
> *That closely by it grew.*

A wandering satyr laments the destruction of the English woodland but is made welcome in Elizium where with the Muses he may sit at pleasure in the shade. Just so Drayton many times grieved for the spoliation of England, as we may, and his distress was genuine enough. But in the last resort what mattered most to him was the transforming power of imagination, the golden world of poetry, not the brazen world of Nature. In his serene old age he would withdraw from all mundane anxieties, and would forgo even his lifelong passion for England and her history the more uninterruptedly to delight in this paradise of the poetic imagination.

Something of this detachment Drayton may have learnt also in his writing of sonnets, for these always countered the prevailing didacticism. He followed his first collection of pastorals with his first sonnets, in the following year, 1594; and again he brought into the title, *Ideas Mirror*, the pastoral name for Anne Goodere, Sir Henry's younger daughter. She had been a baby of eighteen months or so when Drayton entered her father's service, and by now she was in her early twenties. Whether Drayton would have been in love with her, had she been socially within his reach, we cannot tell, but it says much for the character of both of them that they maintained close friendship for more than half a century, from the time when she first knew Drayton as her father's page, through the years of her marriage to Sir Henry Rainsford, when Drayton would stay with them for a month or two at a time at Clifford Chambers, to the day when he died, one of the most famous of English poets. It is in vain therefore to seek in these sonnets for the ardours of a hopeless love affair.

> *Into these loves, who but for passion looks,*
> *At this first sight, here let him lay them by,*
> *And seek elsewhere,*

Drayton advises the reader. True, he added this sonnet in the second edition of 1599 and this advice may be disingenuous, but I think not. Indeed some of the sonnets which most seem to be personal such as

> *Since there's no help, come, let us kiss and part,*

or

> *How many paltry, foolish, painted things,*

first appeared in 1619, in the tenth edition of these poems. All the time Drayton was drastically revising the collection, omitting early poems, adding new, rewriting others, long after other sonneteers of the 1590s had ceased to trouble. He could not leave the form until he had brought it to the greatest excellence of which he was capable.

Like Shakespeare, he was more independent than most of Italian or French models, perhaps because he was ignorant of them ; instead, he drew on his English predecessors Daniel and Lodge at first, with the result that, as Guilpin says, he was 'condemned by some for imitation'. Later, by 1599, he learnt more from Sidney, especially how to combine the high style with the familiar, as he does in the most famous of them all where the direct colloquial address of the octave gives place to the grand personifications of the sestet.

> *Since there's no help, come, let us kiss and part.*
> *Nay, I have done. You get no more of me,*
> *And I am glad, yea, glad with all my heart,*
> *That thus so cleanly I myself can free.*
> *Shake hands for ever ; cancel all our vows ;*
> *And when we meet at any time again*
> *Be it not seen in either of our brows*
> *That we one jot of former love retain.*
> *Now, at the last gasp of Love's latest breath,*
> *When, his pulse failing, Passion speechless lies,*
> *When Faith is kneeling by his bed of death,*

Michael Drayton

And Innocence is closing up his eyes,
Now, if thou wouldst, when all have given him over,
From death to life, thou mightst him yet recover.

He had defied the critics who laughed at the extravagance
of some of his conceits, who accused him of plagiarism, or of
insincerity, but he learnt from them none the less, and with
that devotion to his art which characterized all he did he
went on writing sonnets long after the fashion had ceased.
Here is the same persistence and concentration as in his
treatment of the pastoral form. In the sonnet twenty-five
years of thought and experiment, not some spontaneous over-
flow of powerful feeling, brought him to the perfection of the
poem just quoted.

Pastoral, sonnet — next came Drayton's attempt at another
favourite form of the 1590s, a poem on a classical myth, in
the tradition of Lodge, Shakespeare, and Marlowe. *Endimion and Phoebe* was written for the marriage in December
1594 of Lucy Harington (then not quite fourteen) to the
young Earl of Bedford. The poem was left unfinished,
though not fragmentary, and was published early in 1595.
It is in heroic couplets like *Hero and Leander* and, as Douglas
Bush says, Marlowe's influence 'inspires the creation of more
purely sensuous beauty than Drayton ever achieved again'.
But the poem is not, like Marlowe's or Shakespeare's,
erotic: Endimion is reluctant to love physical beauty in
Phoebe disguised, but in the end is delighted to discover that
after all she is absolute beauty. The poem is thus about the
Platonic conception of love, in which the love aroused by
physical beauty leads to love of divine things. (Had not
Drayton chosen *Idea* for the pastoral name of Anne Goodere
in his pastorals and sonnets?) In particular, the Endymion
myth was taken at the Renaissance to be a symbol of the

origin of man's knowledge of astronomy, and Drayton's poem at the end wanders off (not very convincingly) into these matters. Yet it is clearly, after Shakespeare's and Marlowe's, the best of this kind of poem, and is important in Drayton's work as his first use of the heroic couplet. He never reprinted it, perhaps because, for some unknown reason, he quarrelled with Lady Bedford ; but in 1606 he published a much shorter version, *The Man in the Moone*, in which he made an unsuccessful attempt to convert this idealistic marriage-poem to satire. This was the one kind of poetry which he never tried to develop, perhaps because he recognized that here perfection must remain unattainable for a man with no claim to classical learning.

Besides, the history of England absorbed him as myth could never have done, and here too, as with pastoral, sonnet, and classical epyllion he could work in a tradition that was current at the time. Thus his publication in 1593 or 1594 of the first of his historical poems, *Peirs Gaveston*, shows again his extraordinarily prompt response to the taste of his time. It is almost as if Drayton, determined from childhood to be a poet, was intent on following every example that seemed promising, trying his hand at each of the kinds in turn, in the hope of discovering which best suited his natural gifts.

Drayton did not have the scholarly scepticism or the respect for his sources that led Daniel in the end to turn from historical poem to prose history, with improved success, but he shared Daniel's and Shakespeare's interest in English history. This was part of the Elizabethan national self-consciousness, and of their discovery of England — of the possibilities in the English language, of the beauty of English landscape, of the greatness of England's past in the time of Henry V, of the excitement of living (as they knew they lived) in

England's golden age. So it is that the great bulk of Drayton's work is concerned with the history of England, chiefly in the century and a half before his own time, but with incursions into the further past. Here again he experimented with a variety of ways of writing history, seeking always the method that was most congenial, seeking also the self-knowledge which would allow him to reach an individual excellence and to discover whether he could better manage the spaciousness of epic or the urgency of ballad.

Peirs Gaveston was the first, and longest, of a group of poems which recount the story of a single historical character, to which Drayton gave the name of Legends. The others are *Matilda*, 1594, *Robert of Normandy*, 1596, and *The Legend of Great Cromwell*, 1607. In the address to the reader before *Robert of Normandy* Drayton explains his conception of the form. 'The principle is', he says, 'that being a species of an epic or heroic poem, it eminently describeth the act or acts of some one or other eminent persons.' Like the cautionary tales of the *Mirror for Magistrates* (which Daniel revived in his *Complaint of Rosamond* in 1592) it has a moral : 'to show the world that events are not the measure of counsels, God's pleasure over-swaying in all, for hidden causes'. This is close to the Calvinist view of history, which recognizes the slightness of any one man's influence upon the historical nexus, the workings of Providence. Whether or not Drayton was a follower of Calvin is beside the point, since men may be influenced by fashionable views of history, Calvinist, Hegelian, Marxist, without subscribing to all the other articles of faith.

The choice of a historical subject for the heroic poem was recommended by Tasso, on the grounds that history was more persuasive than myth. If the purpose of the heroic poem was to form the mind to heroic virtue by example

then (the argument ran) men would be more likely to follow
a historical precedent : what men had once done they might
do again. Tasso in basing his greatest poem on the history
of the First Crusade had followed his own precept. Camoens
did the same, selecting with much daring a recent event,
Vasco da Gama's voyage to India, as the subject of *Os
Lusiadas*. Milton rejected the Arthurian cycle of stories,
'*fabled* knights in battles *feigned*', for the more authentic history which he found in *Genesis*. Michael Drayton's contemporary, Samuel Daniel, made the same choice, and even
admitted

I versify the truth, not poetize ;

which is precisely why he is a better historian than historical
poet. We must then think of Drayton's historical poems, as
he did, as 'a species of an epic or heroic poem', in a tradition
then firmly established in western Europe and which led to
the masterpieces of Tasso, Camoens, and Milton.

After the first three *Legends* Drayton wrote, as he hoped, a
'work of greater worth', which was published in 1596 under
the title of *Mortimeriados*. The title suggests that the poem
was of a similar kind to the biographical legends, but it is on
a larger scale and gives Drayton more scope for describing
action, at which (in contrast to Daniel) he was especially good.
In fact the poem is not biographical — Mortimer plays no
great part in it — but rather a narrative of war, in which the
interest is less in individual persons than in events, less,
therefore, in characterization than in narrative. This poem
of almost three thousand lines was Drayton's longest to date ;
but with that indefatigable determination always to make his
poems as good as possible, he entirely rewrote it by 1603
when he published the revised poem, now 3656 lines long,
as *The Barons' Warres*.

This immense labour he undertook for two reasons. The change of title indicates one : he had stood aside, and recognized that the poem was not merely longer than the *Legends* but of a different kind, and he had begun to realize where, in historical writing, his real strength lay. (Perhaps the English were slow to prefer narrative to biography in the heroic poem, for Edward Fairfax entitled his noble translation of Tasso's *Gerusalemme Liberata* in 1600 *Godfrey of Bulloigne*.) Drayton's second motive in rewriting his poem was a technical one, to replace the rhyme royal of *Mortimeriados* with the *ottava rima* of *The Barons' Warres*. He explained his reasons thus : 'Whereas I was advised to write it, and also began it, in the stanza of seven lines . . . the often harmony thereof softened the verse more than the majesty of the subject would permit, unless they had all been couplets (that is, heroic couplets). Therefore . . . I chose this stanza (*ottava rima*), of all other the most complete and best proportioned.' There is more to the same effect, which shows Drayton's intense interest in prosody, his concern with the art of poetry. He was certainly right to prefer this more vigorous stanza, which had helped Ariosto and Tasso and Camoens and many another to their triumphant narratives, instead of the more languid measure of *Troilus and Criseyde*.

This was the largest labour of revision which Drayton ever undertook, but his restless search for perfection led him to revise the three earlier *Legends* several times before they reached their final form in 1619. In 1627 he published two more long historical narratives in *ottava rima*, *The Battle of Agincourt* of some 2500 lines, and *The Miseries of Queen Margarite*, which is a little over 2000 lines. This last shows something of a return to the manner of the *Legends*. The numerous reprintings of all the earlier poems show how great was their popular success in Drayton's lifetime ; but

the most popular of all, then and for long afterwards, were
Englands Heroicall Epistles. The first of these were published
in 1597, and there were twelve more editions before Drayton's death, and one soon afterwards. More unexpectedly
there were further editions in the 1690s, and again in 1737,
when Dryden and Pope were at the height of their fame.

Drayton derived the suggestion for these poems — it is no
more than that — from Ovid's *Heroides*. But whereas Ovid's
poems are nearly all mournful monologues by deserted dam-
sels, taken from ancient myth, Drayton's poems are pairs of
letters exchanged between two lovers known from English
history of the past two centuries. They refer to an immediate
situation, usually towards the end of the affair ; we are made
to understand why the writer of the first letter was impelled
to write at that moment ; the second letter of each pair is a
genuine reply to the first, taking up and answering points
there made. They are thus more dramatic, and less elegiac,
than Ovid's. And because they are concerned with well-
known stories the reader knows what is going to happen
afterwards, and therefore the poet has scope for dramatic
irony.

For the *Epistles* Drayton used the heroic couplet which he
had first attempted in *Endimion and Phoebe*. But he used it
less in the manner of Marlowe, and more in the Augustan
manner, with the end-stopped couplet representing the
elegiac couplet of Ovid. The couplet was suited to the epistolary plain style, as Jonson would later discover, since it did
not, like a more complex stanza, tend to subject matter to
manner. Probably Drayton's use of the couplet, more than
anything else, made these poems acceptable to the Augustan
age ; and as the Elizabethans could find more to their purpose in Surrey than in Wyatt, so the Augustans could find
more in Drayton's *Epistles* than in Donne's.

Elton long ago made a similar point. He quoted these lines :

> *The depth of woe with words we hardly sound ;*
> *Sorrow is so insensibly profound,*

which are from Lady Jane Grey's *Epistle* to Lord Guildford Dudley. 'The placing and cadence of the word *insensibly*' (he says) 'longer and louder than the words about it, are absolute Dryden.' Drayton, already in 1597, could achieve, if only intermittently, the neo-classic manner of a century later. It is proof both of his virtuosity and of his sensibility, for this was perfectly appropriate to the epistolary plain style ; we shall afterwards find him using it in verse letters which he addressed to his friends. Characteristically he developed the manner first in a fictitious, imaginary context before conveying it to his personal use.

Drayton also very soon discovered how readily the heroic couplet accepts antithesis. Lady Geraldine replies to a letter the poet Surrey has written to her from Italy :

> *Till thou return, the Court I will exchange*
> *For some poor cottage, or some country grange,*
> *Where to our distaffs, as we sit and spin,*
> *My maid and I will tell what things have bin,*
> *Our lutes unstrung shall hang upon the wall,*
> *Our lessons serve to wrap our tow withal,*
> *And pass the night, while winter tales we tell,*
> *Of many things that long ago befell,*
> *Or tune such homely carols as were sung*
> *In country sport, when we ourselves were young,*
> *In pretty riddles to bewray our loves,*
> *In questions, purpose, or in drawing gloves . . .*
> *Many of us desire Queen Katharine's state,*
> *But very few her virtues imitate.*

Then, as Ulysses' wife, write I to thee,
Make no reply, but come thyself to me.

In this epistolary form, rather than in extended narrative, Drayton discovered his best means of writing historical poetry. He can draw two characters acting upon one another in all sorts of situations, but he cannot cope so well with the complexity of epic.

There is thus a subtlety of characterization in these poems which he scarcely achieves in the longer ones. There he is so excited about what his men and women are doing that he tends to lose sight of what they were. They are caught in a sequence of events which their own characters seldom seem to motivate. It is the usual defect of the great tellers of tales, and in this Drayton resembles Scott or Byron. But in the simpler situations of the *Epistles* Drayton has time to show his depth of understanding of human character. Besides, in choosing this form he must describe the relations of his two lovers at a moment after the dramatic climax, so that he is not distracted by describing events. Tennyson likewise is much happier in *Ulysses*, or *Oenone*, or *Morte d'Arthur*, where the drama is at an end, than in the *Idylls*, where he is in the midst of it all.

In extreme contrast with the *Epistles* is yet one more kind of historical poem at which Drayton tried his hand, the poem by which he is probably best known, *The Ballad of Agincourt*, first published in 1606. Here he concentrates his outstanding gift for narrative in a poem which is, as it were, stripped for action. It is, besides, a metrical *tour de force*, with the verse beating a tattoo for King Harry and his men with supreme gallantry.

Fair stood the wind for France
When we our sails advance,

Nor now to prove our chance
Longer will tarry.
But putting to the main
At Caux, the mouth of Seine,
With all his martial train
Landed King Harry.

Thus, within a dozen years, Drayton had tried his hand at every kind of historical poem from epic to ballad, from biographical legend to heroical epistle, and had been successful in all. If he could have combined the various qualities he had shown, the narrative vigour of the *Ballad* and the perceptive characterization of the *Epistles*, in one long poem he would have made a third in the company of Spenser and Milton.

With all these varied attempts at writing the heroical poem on English history Drayton was still not content, and during the next years he devoted his immense energy to writing *Poly-Olbion*, of which the first part was published in 1612, and the second in 1622. This is both historical and topographical, a poetical gazetteer of England and Wales, with maps of Saxton and learned notes to the first part by Selden. It runs to nearly fifteen thousand lines, and long twelve-syllabled alexandrines at that. Charles Lamb much admired the poem for both antiquarian and romantic reasons. Drayton (he says) 'has not left a rivulet, so narrow that it may be stepped over, without honourable mention; and has animated hills and streams with life and passion beyond the dreams of old mythology'. The poem is far too long for one which inevitably lacks narrative coherence, though Drayton attempts, by following the course of rivers, to provide some sort of architecture. The way to read it, or to read in it, is the same as with any other guide-book: to take a 'song' (as Drayton perversely terms the different sections of it which no one could dream of singing) that is about a part of the country one knows well, or is visiting — and almost certainly one will find something new, some long-forgotten legend, or a passage of natural description that can still enliven the scene.

The trouble is that Drayton had visited so much of England and Wales, had seen and read so much — he borrowed books from John Stow and William Camden, he used manuscript as well as printed sources — that his poem is a mass of detail which overwhelms the reader. He never gave himself time to stand aside and see the whole shape of England and of her history in perspective. His love of England was too indiscriminate, as if he had discovered it all for the first time. He went everywhere and delighted to record everything, rivers and mountains and moors and fens; history and legend; ruined abbeys, and devastated forests; shepherds and shepherdesses, falconers and fairies; birds, flowers, herbs, crops, cattle. As he himself says,

What subject can be found that lies not fair to me ?
Of simple shepherds now my Muse exactly sings,
And then of courtly loves and the affairs of Kings,
Then, in a buskined strain, the warlike spear and shield,
And instantly again of the disports of field.

In all this, Drayton is at his best, as we should expect, when he is describing what he knows best, the bird-song of the Forest of Arden in his native Warwickshire, the Cotswold shepherds, a flight at brook on the Ouse, or fishing in the fen. His enthusiasm, his industry, and his versatility all alike drove him on to what in the end even he would acknowledge to be 'a strange Herculean toil', and only those who read guide-books from cover to cover are likely to do the same with *Poly-Olbion*. But not many sensible persons altogether disdain either the one or the other.

This inexhaustible energy of Drayton, in writing new poems and revising earlier ones, must most of all astonish us who live in an age when, as has been well said, poems are not expected to be more than wry little footnotes on experience. Drayton was always contemptuous of poetry of that kind, the sort of stuff that Donne and his friends passed round in manuscript but refused to publish, poems that were 'kept in cabinets and must only pass by transcription', as he scornfully remarked in a preface to the first part of *Poly-Olbion*. Drayton must often have been irritated by this fashion, for the younger Sir Henry Goodere (nephew and son-in-law of Drayton's first patron) was for many years Donne's most intimate friend, and no doubt made tactlessly approving comments on his latest poems in Drayton's presence. Drayton must have contrasted the taste of the two Gooderes unfavourably for the younger generation — 'this lunatic age' he growled. It was the usual complaint of the dedicated professional poet, the man who devotes his whole life to poetry, against the frivolous, though gifted, amateur. Ben Jonson said much the same, and so, a century later, did Pope.

Drayton therefore, who otherwise showed so prompt a response to the literary modes and manners of his time, took little from Donne and his kind. Like many other poets of the age, Gascoigne, Spenser, Hall, Donne, Guilpin, Marston, Jonson, he tried his hand at satire, and in *The Owle*, 1604, produced an example whose unintelligibility, notorious in its own day, has been increased by the elucidations of modern scholars. *The Moone-Calfe*, written some time in the second decade of the century, but not published till 1627, is hardly more successful. Drayton's genius, we may conclude, was not destructive; he would often look back nostalgically to the golden age of Elizabeth, and regret the follies of the iron age of James I, but he was not disposed to waste his time in attempts to correct them.

Late in life he devised a much more congenial method of laughing at his contemporaries, in his fairy poem *Nimphidia*. This has claims to be called the first mock-heroic poem in English (unless Spenser's *Muiopotmos* should be preferred), and it has always been one of the best known of all Drayton's works. It derives much from *A Midsummer Night's Dream*, but Drayton has a freedom denied there to Shakespeare, in that he can diminish the scale of his fairies as Mercutio could diminish Queen Mab, but as Shakespeare could not diminish Oberon and Titania. The hero, Pigwiggen, has a secret assignation with the fairy Queen, Mab, and, being sought by the jealous King, Oberon, girds himself for the encounter, and mounts his gallant steed.

> *Himself he on an earwig set,*
> *Yet scarce he on his back could get,*
> *So oft and high he did curvet*
>   *Ere he himself could settle.*
> *He made his turn, and stop, and bound,*
> *To gallop, and to trot the round ;*
> *He scarce could stand on any ground,*
>   *He was so full of mettle.*

The lively metre looks back to the Sir Thopas stanza which Drayton had used long before for the *Ballad of Dowsabell* in his earliest pastorals, but now the use of feminine rhyme in the fourth and eighth lines lifts and lightens it to match the tone of the poem. It is yet another example of Drayton's metrical tact and invention.

This may be seen again in the collection of short poems published in 1606 to which Drayton gave the name of *Odes*. (The term had only once before been used in this way in

English, by Soowthern in his clod-hopping imitations of Ronsard in 1584.) There is a remarkable variety in these twenty poems, of which the *Ballad of Agincourt* is the most famous. Besides this 'old English garb' of ballad, as Drayton calls it, he wrote Skeltonics, which is no less surprising at the time; he wrote a song *To his Coy Love* which might have been written by a Cavalier thirty years later, and one or two, *The Heart*, *The Cryer*, which have something of the earlier 'metaphysical' manner. The odes show Drayton's extraordinary versatility, his readiness to attempt almost every manner, current or out of date, and his success in doing so. What other poet of his time, or of any time, would include in the same volume poems as different as *The Ballad of Agincourt*, *A Skeltoniad*, *The Heart* and *To his Coy Love*? This:

> *The Muse should be sprightly,*
> *Yet not handling lightly*
> *Things grave; as much loth*
> *Things that be slight to clothe*
> *Curiously. To retain*
> *The comeliness in mean*
> *Is true knowledge and wit.*

And this:

> *If thus we needs must go,*
> *What shall our one heart do,*
> *This one made of our two?*
>
> *Madame, two hearts we brake,*
> *And from them both did take*
> *The best, one heart to make.*
>
> *Half this is of your heart,*
> *Mine in the other part,*
> *Joined by our equal art.*

And this :

> *I pray thee leave, love me no more,*
>   *Call home the heart you gave me,*
> *I but in vain that saint adore*
>   *That can, but will not, save me.*
> *These poor half kisses kill me quite ;*
> *Was ever man thus served ?*
> *Amidst an ocean of delight*
>   *For pleasure to be starved.*

In his preface Drayton notes the ambiguity of the term Ode, which can include poems by Pindar and 'Anacreon' and Horace. He does not claim any of these as his model, but contents himself with saying that his poems are new, 'and the work of playing hours'. He dedicated them to the younger Sir Henry Goodere in verses which recall songs sung by the fireside at his house at Polesworth. Perhaps, at the back of his mind, was some thought of competing with those evaporations of Donne's wit which must often have pleased the same company in their playing hours, but did not much please him.

Some of these odes, in spite of Drayton's disclaimer, suggest, for the first time in English, the Odes of Horace. Drayton's *Elegies* again follow Horace, or rather Ben Jonson's adaptation of Horace's familiar, epistolary manner of the *Sermones* which is very different from the concinnity of the Odes. (At the time Horace, to English readers, still meant the writer of the Satires and Epistles and *De Arte Poetica*, not the writer of the Odes. That came later, in the Augustan age.) Of Drayton's *Elegies* seven are verse letters to his friends, and five are funerary poems. They are in heroic couplets, and what could more exactly suggest Pope's *Epistle to Dr. Arbuthnot* than Drayton's poem *To Henry Reynolds* ?

My dearly loved friend, how oft have we
In winter evenings (meaning to be free)
To some well chosen place used to retire,
And there, with moderate meat, and wine, and fire,
Have passed the hours contentedly with chat,
Now talked of this, and then discoursed of that ;
Spoke our own verses 'twixt ourselves, if not
Other men's lines, which we by chance had got,
Or some stage pieces, famous long before,
Of which your happy memory had store.

This is the poem in which Drayton recounts his childish ambition to be a poet, and then goes on to give those generous and succinct summaries of the poets of his own day and before which we still so assiduously quote. He ends with a characteristic dig at Donne and his like who will not subject their poems to public censure by having them printed ; but the whole poem is instinct with Drayton's unwavering devotion to the art of poetry. No one, not Spenser certainly nor Milton, not even Jonson or Dryden or Pope, has ever been a more dedicated poet than Michael Drayton.

But, as the *Epistle to Henry Reynolds* shows, he was a friendly, clubbable man, one who enjoyed talking about poets and poetry with his friends, in Ben Jonson's *Apollo* room at the Devil and St Dunstan, when he was in London ; at Polesworth Hall when he was visiting Sir Henry Goodere, or at Clifford Chambers when he was there for summer holidays with Sir Henry and Lady Rainsford – Anne Goodere that was, the Idea of his earliest inspiration, and his most constant friend through life. The Rainsfords' family doctor was John Hall (who married Shakespeare's daughter Susanna), and he tells us that in her sixties Lady Rainsford was 'modest, pious, kind and deserving well of everybody, much given to reading the scriptures, and skilled in French and Italian'. Drayton's ironical self-portrait as the weary old satyr who intrudes into the *Muses Elizium* and startles the nymphs there, is contemporary. And surely it is fitting that, on the last evening of a life that had been so truly all of one piece, his mind returned to those early days when, as a little village boy, he had come to her father's house, and that he should address his last verses to Anne Goodere, whom he had known and loved for sixty years.

> *The seeds of love first by thy eyes were thrown*
> *Into a ground untilled, a heart unknown*
> *To bear such fruit, till by thy hands 'twas sown.*

> *Look, as your looking-glass by chance may fall,*
> *Divide and break in many pieces small,*
> *And yet shows forth the self-same face in all, —*

> *Proportions, features, graces just the same,*
> *And in the smallest piece as well the name*
> *Of fairest one deserves, as in the richest frame ;*

> *So all my thoughts are pieces but of you,*
> *Which, put together, make a glass so true*
> *As I therein no other's face but yours can view.*

TEXTS

Works, ed. J. W. Hebel, 5 vols. (vol. 5, ed. Kathleen Tillotson and B. H. Newdigate), Oxford, Shakespeare Head Press, 1931-41, reprinted 1961.

Poems, ed. John Buxton, 2 vols. (Muses' Library), Routledge & Kegan Paul, 1953.

Edmund Waller

5

EDMUND WALLER

EDMUND WALLER was born on 3 March 1606 at the
manor house of Coleshill in Hertfordshire, the eldest
son of a rich and unambitious country gentleman who, at his
death ten years later, regretted that he had led so idle a life.
Through his mother Waller was first cousin to a country
gentleman of notable vigour, John Hampden (and so also
connected with Cromwell), but in his own character there
seems to have been more of the easy-going refinement of his
father than of the robust efficiency of his mother. His character has been much abused, and with some justice, though
in an age of fanatical partisanship there may be something to
be said for the man whose cool and passionless temper allows
no irrevocable loyalty. 'Coward' and 'traitor' many called
him ; but he had the wit to shrug the insults off, as on the
famous occasion when King Charles objected that the poem
Waller had just written on his Restoration was less ardent
than his earlier panegyric on Cromwell. 'Sir,' Waller
replied, 'we poets succeed better in fiction than in truth.'
When men's factious souls were wearied into peace such an
answer satisfied most critics.

Whatever our estimate of Waller's character, it cannot be
denied that to his successors, Dryden, Pope, and the rest, he
was the most celebrated lyrical poet of the century. He lived
through more than eighty years of it, from soon after the
accession of James I to shortly before the dismissal of James

II ; and for sixty of those years he was writing his urbane, delightful verses. Throughout, his style changed so little that (as men said) 'were we to judge only by the wording, we could not know what was wrote at twenty, and what at fourscore'.

It is unlikely that Waller will ever again hold so high a place among the English poets as that where the Augustans installed him ; but since the men who so much admired him were not only fine poets but critics of much learning and judgment, we may pause to reconsider the poems on which that reputation was based. The opinion that Waller first used the heroic couplet in the manner of Dryden or Pope is easily disproved : Drayton, Sir John Beaumont, and George Sandys (and not only they) often achieved the desired Ovidian polish. But these historical discoveries can be misleading. Dryden's judgment of Waller is more significant for the history of poetry than any modern assertion of what that judgment ought to have been. The task of a true historical criticism must be to discover why the Augustans admired Waller as they did, not to show that they were wrong to do so.

John Aubrey, who knew Waller, tells us that when, as a brisk young spark, he first studied poetry, 'Methought', said he, 'I never saw a good copy of English verses ; they want smoothness ; then I began to essay.' 'Smoothness,' then, was the quality he wished to achieve and for which he was especially praised. This was something more than mere fluency — rather the formal precision and elegant completeness of the Latin elegiac couplet. So, when Waller writes a compliment to Lady Morton, he writes as a poet of Augustan Rome would have written, had he known English :

> *Madam ! new years may well expect to find*
> *Welcome from you, to whom they are so kind ;*

> *Still as they pass, they court and smile on you,*
> *And make your beauty, as themselves, seem new.*

The poem was written for New Year's day 1650 when he and she were sharing the Royalists' exile in Paris, along with Davenant and Cowley and Hobbes. A few years later he celebrated a naval victory over Spain in a similar manner :

> *Others may use the ocean as their road,*
> *Only the English make it their abode,*
> *Whose ready sails with every wind can fly,*
> *And make a covenant with the inconstant sky ;*
> *Our oaks secure, as if they there took root.*
> *We tread on billows with a steady foot.*

The manner is, for us at least, all too similar, since what is appropriate in a witty compliment to a Court beauty cannot be equally appropriate to a description of battle at sea in which the Parliamentary fleet was victorious. Yet, when the poem was published in Carrington's *Life of Cromwell*, 1659, the author was called 'the English Virgil of our times', which suggests that contemporaries detected no such inadequacy. Certainly Waller's couplets invite any reader familiar with Latin to translate them at once : he achieves to perfection, if not the Virgilian, then certainly the Ovidian style.

But (we may ask) why should this be thought a merit ? Why, after the immense achievement of the Elizabethans, should an English poet still choose to rely on a classical tradition ? Waller himself gives the answer in his poem *Of English Verse*.

> *But who can hope his lines should long*
> *Last in a daily changing tongue ?*
> *While they are new, envy prevails ;*
> *And as that dies, our language fails . . .*

Poets that lasting marble seek
Must carve in Latin or in Greek
We write in sand ; our language grows,
And, like the tide, our work o'erflows.

Chaucer his sense can only boast ;
The glory of his numbers lost !

We forget that Waller, like Spenser or Dryden, was bewildered by Chaucer's metre. Yet, recognizing in him a great English poet, they inquired how they might guarantee that their own language and metre should not become obsolete in a century and a half, as Chaucer's had done. For Waller Sir Francis Kynaston's recent translation of *Troilus and Criseyde* into Latin rhyme royal was not a piece of academic virtuosity but a generous attempt (as Kynaston intended) to make Chaucer's poetry *per omnia secula stabilem et immotum*. They could not detect that English itself had become more stabilized, and even Pope feared that the time would soon come when

Our sons their father's failing language see,
And such as Chaucer is, shall Dryden be.

Besides, they did not think of a continuing evolution of language, as we do. Latin for them was not a 'dead' language, in which this process had ceased : it was a language that had reached its term of perfection, and which therefore ought to be imitated not only by those who wrote Latin but (so far as possible) by those who wrote in other languages. Bembo's classicism in Italy had been of this kind ; so in England was Waller's or Milton's. Believing as they did that languages could be perfected they necessarily wished to bring English to perfection in their own writings. This Waller set out to do, and this the Augustans believed he had

done. 'The tongue came into his hands like a rough dia-
mond : he polished it first, and to that degree, that all artists
since have admired the workmanship, without pretending to
mend it. . . . He undoubtedly stands first in the list of
refiners, and, for aught I know, last too ; for I question
whether in Charles II's reign English did not come to its full
perfection ; and whether it has not had its Augustan age as
well as the Latin.'

Now the whole conception of language implied in these
words of Francis Atterbury may seem to us erroneous and
absurd, but we can hardly hope to appreciate the poetry of
the time unless we understand them. The poets, as the
greatest among them said, were eager 'to leave something so
written to aftertimes as they should not willingly let it die'.
'Something *so written*' Milton would have emphasized, for
he knew that it was the quality of the writing more than anything else that must insure the survival of his poetry. Atterbury, in another passage, suggests that this was also Waller's
purpose. 'He sought out, in this flowing tongue of ours,
what parts would last, and be of standing use and ornament' ;
and again (referring to the lines *Of English Verse* which I have
just quoted) 'though English be mouldering stone, as he tells
us there, yet he has certainly picked the best out of a bad
quarry'. This was how his contemporaries saw his achievement, and if, like Surrey, he is remembered now principally
for his enormous influence on poets greater than himself, yet
his own poems deserve to be read. As Mr Eliot has pointed
out, great poets sometimes need supplementing by good
ones, and beyond question Waller was a good poet, who
ought to be known for more than the two or three exquisite
songs that are to be found in dozens of anthologies. Indeed,
it is odd that a poet who was once chiefly praised for his use
of the heroic couplet should now be most often quoted in

other measures. We no longer wish to write heroic couplets, but Dryden and the Augustans saw in this the perfect form for the poetry that they wished to write. They believed that they could learn more from Waller than from any other poet, for

> *His happy genius did our tongue refine,*
> *And easy words with pleasing numbers join.*

Dryden admired Chaucer and Spenser and Milton, but none of these could help him to write his own poetry. For that he must turn to Waller.

There is in Waller's poetry no passion, no profound concern with the disputes and controversies of the age. He spent many years as a Member of Parliament, to which he was first elected at the age of sixteen, and he gained there the reputation of a brilliant and witty speaker who savoured the distinction of his own eloquence more than the forceful advocacy of a cause. He was, he observed, with a gentlemanly litotes, 'impatient of the inconvenience of the war', but he had none of the bitter regret that drove his friend Lord Falkland to seek death in battle. Like that other poet and member of Parliament, Andrew Marvell, he wished for compromise, and was too sophisticated to think any cause worth fighting for. He was rich and accomplished and preferred to spend a whole summer polishing ten lines to write in the Duchess of York's Tasso to what the world, then as now, called 'more serious employments'. He never needed to fawn for patronage, nor to be subservient to any man's judgment : he wrote, as he said, 'only to please himself and such particular persons to whom his poems were directed'. Faults of character he might have, but faults of manners never ; and his charm, we are told, 'was of magnitude enough to cover a world of very great faults'. In a book of

verses published in his memory one of his friends paid him
the perfect compliment :

He tuned the company wheree'er he came.

Waller himself could not have improved on this. His taste
was impeccable : he never descended to coarseness or ob-
scenity ; he preferred paying compliments to uttering invec-
tive ; was pious without being effusive, and abstemious
without being censorious. Henry Savile was once heard to
say that 'no man in England should keep him company without drinking but Ned Waller' ; and those who were privileged to enjoy his friendship gladly forgave him defects still
more reprehensible.

Most of his poems he addressed to those friends, ladies
and gentlemen of the Court or the country, in compliment,
congratulation, or condolence. They illustrate the formal
manners of polite society in the seventeenth century, and are
never intimate, not even when he addresses Sacharissa, the
Lady Dorothy Sidney with whom he is said to have been
passionately in love. Perhaps he was, though his nature was
affectionate rather than passionate ; but he would no more
have made such an admission in published verses than he
would have embraced her in a public place. To have done
so would have been unthinkably vulgar, and therefore dis-
gusting to them both. He was vain enough to compare himself to Phoebus courting Daphne, since

> *what he sung in his immortal strain,*
> *Though unsuccessful was not sung in vain ;*
> *All, but the nymph that should redress his wrong,*
> *Attend his passion, and approve his song.*
> *Like Phoebus thus, acquiring unsought praise,*
> *He catched at love, and filled his arm with bays.*

We are left to suppose that this was what he preferred ; that he was less interested in Lady Dorothy who lived at Penshurst, than in Sacharissa, who inhabited the more fashionable world of his verses. To a Romantic this may seem disappointing, but to the Age of Taste it was acceptable. 'Waller is not always at the last gasp ; he does not die of a frown, nor live upon a smile.' Dr Johnson, being a sensible man, was grateful.

Waller never, like Donne, raises his voice to attract our attention, never tries to shock or startle by an impromptu extravagance of wit. He has no message to the world, unless it is of the charm of good manners and the pleasure of gay company. He is indifferent to the causes that disturb and stultify mankind. He cares about good verses as an adjunct of civilized living, just as he cares about Van Dyck's painting, and fine clothes, and keeping a good table, and handsome women. 'Her presence', he wrote of Sacharissa,

> *has such more than human grace,*
> *That it can civilize the rudest place.*

His judgment of life is aesthetic, not moral or political : as such not necessarily incongruous in a poet.

Because this was so, he never attempted poems outside the range of his gifts. Like Jane Austen he had a clear understanding of what this was, and was content to do well what he knew he could do — to do these things as well, indeed, as they have ever been done. He was not ambitious to write a heroic poem, to portray some noble example of man's moral energy for the instruction of his fellows ; where he comes nearest to this, in his longest poem, he provides *Instructions to a Painter* and so shifts the obligation elsewhere. He disdained satire because, in his opinion, such wit was available to those who required it, at Billingsgate. 'The cursed earth naturally produces briars and thorns and weeds, but roses and fine flowers require cultivation.' As a country gentleman he enjoyed cultivating his roses.

Whether it was to Sacharissa or to some other young lady that he sent a rose which he plucked one day in his garden together with a copy of verses he had written for her, we cannot say, though there is a miniature of Lady Dorothy at Penshurst, dressed in a blue gown and with a white rose in her hair. It matters very little, for the exquisite verses are as fresh as on the day when he wrote them.

> *Go, lovely Rose !*
> *Tell her that wastes her time and me*
> *That now she knows,*
> *When I resemble her to thee,*
> *How sweet and fair she seems to be.*
>
> *Tell her that's young,*
> *And shuns to have her graces spied,*
> *That hadst thou sprung*
> *In deserts, where no men abide,*
> *Thou must have uncommended died.*
>
> *Small is the worth*
> *Of beauty from the light retired ;*
> *Bid her come forth,*
> *Suffer herself to be desired,*
> *And not blush so to be admired.*
>
> *Then die ! that she*
> *The common fate of all things rare*
> *May read in thee ;*
> *How small a part of time they share*
> *That are so wondrous sweet and fair !*

Surely Dr Johnson was unjust to deny pathos to Waller : he was as conscious as any poet that beauty vanishes, beauty passes, that brightness falls from the air. The only unkind remark of his that has been recorded derives from his appreciation of the transience of beauty, even of Sacharissa's. The old Countess of Sunderland (as she then was) meeting him one day asked him when he would again write for her verses such as he had once written. 'When you are as young, Madam, and as handsome as you were then.' Perhaps we may find, in the sudden asperity of this answer, more certain evidence of his passion for her than he ever admitted to those verses. For at last the greatest beauties whom Van Dyke or he had praised in their youth must surrender to the impertinence of years.

> *Had Helen, or the Egyptian Queen,*
> *Been ne'er so thrifty of their graces,*
> *Those beauties must at length have been*
> *The spoil of age, which finds out faces*
> *In the most retired places.*

He who lived so long that Lady Sunderland would refer to him in the disparaging tones of long familiarity as 'old Waller', was aware always of the quick passing of youth, and made it the theme of *Go, lovely Rose!*, of that delicate and witty compliment to Lady Morton, of the gallant and tender address *To a very young Lady*.

> *Why came I so untimely forth*
> *Into a world which, wanting thee,*
> *Could entertain us with no worth*
> *Or shadow of felicity,*
> *That time should me so far remove*
> *From that which I was born to love ?*

(She was Lucy, a younger sister of Dorothy Sidney, and later married a Pelham.) But a hint of sadness is not an essential ingredient in poetry, and Waller, who could unite in one line, as in one room, the gay, the wise, the gallant, and the grave, had a general preference, we may suppose, for the gallant and the gay, and wrote more for them than for the wise and grave.

He was disposed to comment on the improvements in St James's Park effected by King Charles at his Restoration, on the Queen's enlargement of Somerset House, on Le Sueur's noble statue of King Charles I at Charing Cross. He wrote, as other poets had written, of Penshurst where Sir Philip Sidney had been born, and where Lady Dorothy lived ; of a lady walking in a garden, or playing the lute, or coming up to London from the country, or (more improbably) playing with a snake. He addressed a few poets, Ben Jonson, George Sandys, Sir William Davenant, Sir John Suckling, Sir William Killigrew, all of them very different from himself in character and as poets. He recognized the cruel dilemma with which civil war had confronted Falkland's great soul ; and he complimented John Evelyn, with whom he visited Italy and Switzerland, on his translation of Lucretius. Of himself he revealed almost nothing. There was no need, for they all knew him, and had his verses by heart, especially those to Sacharissa, so that long afterwards Steele could lament the declining age in which he lived by reference to her. 'The fine women they show me nowadays are at best but pretty girls to me, who have seen Sacharissa, when all the world repeated the poems she inspired .. . . They tell me I am old. I am glad I am so, for I do not like your present young ladies.' Besides, Waller preferred the well mannered remoteness of social intercourse to the intimacies of self-revelation ; the applauded eloquence, not the embattled controversies, of the House of Commons ; the smooth finish of English couplets, not the strong lines that lingered in fashion when he was young. He could not write verses whenever he chose, he told Aubrey, 'but when the fit comes upon him, he does it easily'. There may be a hint of idleness here, but also a recognition that he must be in the mood if he would pay the perfect compliment, or make the finished riposte. Such refined dilettantism (if that is what it was) is out of fashion in this grave and ill-mannered age ; the more's the pity.

Great art, said Kant, has no time for mere charm. This may be true, but many of us even now, are happy enough when on occasion we find ourselves in its company. To Dr Johnson elegance and gaiety were the characteristics of Waller's poetry, and surely they are not so common with us that we can afford their neglect. For their presentation Waller perfected the instrument of the heroic couplet. When in his youth he was a member of Lord Falkland's circle at Great Tew the heroic couplet came much under discussion. George Sandys fashioned it with deft skill for his translation of the *Metamorphoses*, and Lord Falkland himself also showed his mastery of the form while confessing his admiration for Ovid.

> *Next Ovid calls me ; which, though I admire*
> *For equalling the author's quickening fire,*
> *And his pure phrase ; yet more, remembering it*
> *Was by a mind so much distracted writ :*
> *Business and war, ill mid-wives to produce*
> *The happy off-spring of so sweet a muse.*

Falkland's verse is more vigorous and masculine than Waller's, and he is more adventurous in risking the disruption of the couplet pattern. But, as in the last line quoted, there is the characteristic parallelism between the two halves of the line, which became so important to Waller and his successors, and there is a readiness to avoid too great a number of monosyllables which, as Pope pointed out, can be destructive of the smoothness of the ten-syllable line. Francis Atterbury attributed this improvement to Waller, and saw that he was also ingenious in contriving that syntactical and metrical pattern should coincide and so reinforce each other. But he was careful to prevent the monotony which, in so narrow a form as the couplet, might easily result from this.

In his mock-heroic *Battle of the Summer Islands* Waller describes those paradisal islands, the Bermudas ;

> *For the kind spring, which but salutes us here,*
> *Inhabits there, and courts them all the year.*
> *Ripe fruits and blossoms on the same trees live ;*
> *At once they promise what at once they give.*
> *So sweet the air, so moderate the clime,*
> *None sickly lives, or dies before his time.*
> *Heaven sure has kept this spot of earth uncursed*
> *To show how all things were created first.*

The couplets are all enclosed, but within that restricted space he varies the pattern with admirable subtlety. In the first couplet a parenthesis, running over into the second line, interposes between subject and verb, and the contrast between 'but salutes' and 'inhabits' is marked by the contrast between the strong stress on 'inhabits' at the beginning of the second line and the light stress on 'but salutes' in the penultimate place in the first line. In the second couplet the second line repeats the idea of the first in abstract for concrete terms, and has the characteristic antithesis between its two halves emphasized by the repetition of 'at once'. A similar parallelism in the first line of the third couplet is

matched in the second line, but there the chiasmic arrangement (adverb-verb, verb-adverbial phrase) makes a pleasing
variation. The fourth couplet unites the two lines into a
continuous sentence. This is the perfect metrical form for
such gay mockery, as Pope well knew.

Yet Waller's poetry is not always trivial. When he
praises Cromwell he does so without loss of dignity, with no
venality, and though Hazlitt's praise of the poem derives, in
part, from his Republican sympathies — it was, he said,
'serious and sublime' — King Charles himself detected its
merit. Cromwell was of Waller's kindred, and enjoyed the
vivacity of his conversation as a relaxation from the long-
winded haranguing of the Saints ; but Waller, like Marvell,
recognized Cromwell's greatness, and saw that, at least for a
time, Cromwell's government was in England's best interests.
His panegyric is therefore, beyond all else, a patriotic poem,
stately, restrained, in no way obsequious. His own political
conduct was not always dignified, and he was no upholder of
systems, but he could praise in others the qualities he himself lacked.

At the end of his life, when over eighty and no longer able
to read or to write, he could still compose poetry as polite as
ever, but proof (if any were needed) that he was not merely
the gifted playboy of Clarendon's portrait. Confronted by
death he could look back over his life and acknowledge its
failures :

> For then we know how vain it was to boast
> Of fleeting things, so certain to be lost.
> Clouds of affection from our younger eyes
> Conceal that emptiness which age descries.
>   The soul's dark cottage, battered and decayed,
>   Lets in new light through chinks that time has made ;

Stronger by weakness, wiser men become
As they draw near to their eternal home.
Leaving the old, both worlds at once they view,
That stand upon the threshold of the new.

This is not the confession of a frivolous, vain man, used to relying on his personal charm to circumvent the awkwardness of life ; neither is it the prescribed repentance for a life of dissipation. He retained his vivacity and charm, St-Évremond wrote, into old age, and still

S'attache à la beauté pour vivre plus long temps.

He had inherited something of his mother's good sense and resolution, and need not, like his father, regret a wasted life. He had learnt to value his own gifts dispassionately, and in extreme old age had come to see more clearly truths that the affectionate partiality of youth had concealed. The wise and the grave, as well as the gallant and the gay, had made him what he was.

TEXT

Poems, ed. G. Thorn-Drury, 2 vols. (Muses' Library), Routledge & Kegan Paul, 1893.

6

SIR RICHARD FANSHAWE

SIR RICHARD FANSHAWE was a courtier and scholar in the High Renaissance tradition, with a gift for writing poetry which he occasionally revealed in original poems graceful enough to make us wish there had been more, but which he normally chose to subject to the more powerful genius of Virgil or Horace, Guarini or Camoens. He was a linguist of distinction at a time when this was a less rare (because more necessary) accomplishment than it has now become, and he could translate from Latin and Italian, from Spanish and Portuguese, with equal fluency. Appropriately, in view of this capacity for languages, he was employed by both King Charles I and King Charles II on diplomatic missions, but much of his more arduous work of translation was done while he was unemployed during the Interregnum.

He was born in June 1608 at Ware Park in Hertfordshire, the fifth son of Sir Henry Fanshawe and of his wife Elizabeth, a daughter of the redoubtable Customer Smythe. His grandfather had bought the property, famous especially for its noble gardens, some thirty years before, a generation after his family had ambitiously moved South from Derbyshire. Sir Henry was the third Fanshawe to hold the Court appointment of King's Remembrancer of the Exchequer, which several other members of the family, including Sir Richard, were to hold in their turn, and he had been knighted by King James shortly after his accession to the English throne. Sir

Henry died when Richard was a child of seven, and his education therefore devolved upon the care of his capable mother. She sent him to the well-known school kept by Thomas Farnaby who encouraged him to try his hand at poetry, perhaps (as many a later schoolmaster has done) by inviting him to make versions from Virgil or Horace or Ovid. In 1623 Richard went up to Jesus College, Cambridge. Three years later he was entered of the Inner Temple, but he found the Law 'disagreeable to his inclination' and on his mother's death in 1631 abandoned studies which he had endured only to please her.

He had already shown his gifts as a poet. It is likely that some of the translations from Horace, which he eventually published in 1652, are among his earliest work. In translating from the Odes he made some skilful experiments in metrical form with the purpose of representing, rather than reproducing, in English accentual measures Alcaics, Sapphics, and Asclepiads. He rejected earlier attempts to naturalize quantitative prosody in English, but he had so just an understanding of both languages that he could invent stanzas which would convey to an English ear the pattern of their Latin originals. He used these new stanzas also for poems that were not translated, as in two Odes written not later than 1630. The first of these he headed with the motto of uncertain (but not classical) origin which Sir Philip Sidney had first attached to one of his sonnets : *Splendidis longum valedico nugis*. In it he bids farewell to the Muse and promises to run to the Law as a more suitable profession for a younger son, as he had no doubt often been advised. He would never have made any such promise after his mother's death. The Ode is in the Horatian manner, and is written in that English substitute for the Alcaic stanza which Fanshawe used for his versions of half a dozen of Horace's Odes. This is

the same stanza which Marvell borrowed twenty years later
to celebrate Cromwell's return from Ireland, and though it is
impossible to suggest where Marvell had seen Fanshawe's
poems, we can hardly doubt that he had. Poems then circulated widely enough in manuscript, and the opening stanza
of Marvell's Ode echoes even in theme, as well as in prosody,
the opening stanza of Fanshawe's Ode.

> *Ye vanities of human race,*
> *That lead fond youth the wild-goose-chase,*
> *Mindless of after good,*
> *Be gone ! Ye are understood !*

It seems likely therefore that Marvell not only knew of Fanshawe's stanza in versions of Horace, but that he had seen
this poem, which was not published until our own day. Thus
to Fanshawe belongs the credit for inventing a form which
better than any other allowed Marvell to convey into English
the *curiosa felicitas* of Horace himself.

Another poem of the same date touches on this same subject of the conflict between study of the Law and the wish to
write poetry. This is in Fanshawe's adaptation of the
Sapphic stanza.

> *My quenched and discontinued Muse*
> *Her idle fires again renews,*
> *Which from my course do me withdraw —*
> *The thriving Law.*

But in spite of personal ambition and the pleading of friends
he cannot give up writing poetry.

> *I would not (fair) spin out my brains*
> *In rhyme ; this breast such work disdains,*
> *And something that to worth aspires*
> *Faintly desires ;*

Which makes me hate the Thespian springs
That train me from more solid things :
No fruits to show of all my hours, —
   Only some flowers.

But Phoebus pulls me by the arm
And, 'Fool,' quoth he, 'Who does thee harm ?
Trees have, that fruit in autumn bring,
   Their flowers in spring.'

There are awkwardnesses here which suggest immaturity, but enough talent to show how impossible it would be for Richard Fanshawe ever to forgo for long the pleasures of poetry. As Lady Fanshawe told their son, 'He never used exercise but walking, and that generally with some book in his hand, which oftentimes was poetry'.

For such a man the retired life of the country must always have seemed preferable to the busy life of the city, the private life of a cultivated gentleman to the public duty of a courtier. So when, on 9 September 1630, King Charles issued yet another in a long series of Proclamations 'commanding the gentry to reside upon their estates in the Country', Fanshawe found a theme entirely congenial to the Horatian manner of his choice. Again he uses his adapted Sapphic stanza, but with more fluent ease, and he praises country life in the tradition of *Beatus ille, qui procul negotiis*. . . . The poem gains in dignity through the contrast which he draws, as many an Elizabethan had drawn, between the peace of England and the turmoil of the Continent, then in the midst of the Thirty Years War.

  Now war is all the world about,
  And everywhere Erinnys reigns,
  Or else the torch so late put out
   The stench remains.

Holland for many years hath been
Of Christian tragedies the stage,
Yet seldom hath she played a scene
　　Of bloodier rage.

And France, that was not long composed,
With civil drums again resounds,
And ere the old are fully closed
　　Receives new wounds.

Wherever he looked in Europe there was the same bloodshed and savagery, whereas in England there was still peace.

Only the island which we sow
(A world without the world) so far
From present wounds, it cannot show
　　An ancient scar.

White Peace (the beautifullest of things)
Seems here her everlasting rest
To fix, and spreads her downy wings
　　Over the nest.

As when great Jove, usurping reign,
From the plagued world did her exile
And tied her with a golden chain
　　To one blest isle.

He concludes his poem with the familiar contrast, such as Spenser had often made, between the corrupt and hypocritical life of the city and the happy, easy innocence of country life, that perennial English theme (as it had been Virgil's and Horace's) however variously different generations treat it. For whereas in other nations men who win success move into town and buy their town houses, in England the tendency has always been the reverse, as Thomas

Sprat, for example, noted shortly after the Restoration. Most of us sympathize instinctively with Sir Thomas Wyatt's preference for Kent and Christendom, or with Charles Cotton's nostalgia for Beresford Hall ; and a rhetorical question is therefore apt to Fanshawe's poem because for an Englishman there could be but one answer.

> *Who would pursue*
> *The smoky glory of the town*
> *That may go till his native earth,*
> *And by the shining fire sit down*
> *Of his own hearth ?*

There are not many more poems that can be dated to these early years when Fanshawe was still tied to his study of the Law. He was a more dutiful son than George Gascoigne (whose dislike of the Law was no less than his), more modest and cautious. Apart from some of the translations from Horace — and it should be remarked that Fanshawe was much ahead of his time in preferring the Odes to the Satires and Epistles — he translated some of the epigrams of Martial, and most of the verses from Boethius's *De Consolatione Philosophiae*, whose long popularity was drawing to its close. One other poem which, like the *Ode on his Majesty's Proclamation*, was occasioned by public events, dates from late in 1632, the poem *On the report of four Kings dead at once*. Gustavus Adolphus was killed at Lutzen 16 November 1632, and the Elector Frederick of Bohemia died on the 29th : Fanshawe names them both, but it is uncertain who were the two other Kings reported dead. Perhaps, since he does not name them, he doubted the reports.

Not many months later Richard Fanshawe was in Spain. For, in spite of the disturbed condition of the Continent, in spite of a preference for life at home, a young man must travel to enlarge his education. His mother's death had released him from those legal studies which he had loyally endured for nearly five years and he was free to travel, first to Paris and afterwards to Spain where he was to spend most of the next five years. He learnt the language and began to read and to translate Spanish poetry, and he also had his first experience of diplomacy, with the Earl of Bedford and afterwards with Lord Aston. Both ambassadors would have been sympathetic to Fanshawe's literary interests. Lord Bedford must have known the wife of the cousin whom he had just succeeded, Lucy the brightness of the poets' sphere, patron of Daniel and Drayton, of Jonson and Donne. Lord Aston was himself the author of verses which in his own day had some reputation, and for three generations in the seventeenth century his family wrote, transcribed, and collected poems. He would have expected a young man of good breeding to try his hand at poetry and, as the one time patron of Michael Drayton (whom he invited to accompany him as his squire to King James's Coronation) he would have had the critical judgment to approve what Fanshawe wrote.

One of the poems written at this time was that on *The Escorial*, Philip II's vast palace and monastery at Madrid. Poems on houses are frequent in the seventeenth century, but these are usually of country houses belonging to the poet's patron and are thus more intimate than a description of a foreign royal palace could be. Fanshawe was less interested in the architecture than in the collection of pictures which the palace contained, and to these he devoted most of his poem. Of them all Titian's *Magdalene* most impressed him, with its sensuous and dramatic beauty.

> *How well the painter to the life expressed*
> *The soft and swelling ivory of her breast !*

Her flashing cheeks ! Her long bright hair unrolled
And spilt upon the ground like molten gold ! *
But oh ! her tears ! and could he paint them too ?
(A sinner wished them his, they seemed so true.)

An interest in painting was not uncommon in poets of the
time, as may be seen in the work of many of them, from
Sidney and Donne (who owned a Titian) to Cotton and Lady
Winchilsea.

Fanshawe came home on leave at least three times during
these years in Spain. In August 1636 while he was back in
England he went to stay with Lord Aston's daughters,
Gertrude and Constantia, at Colton, a property of Lord
Aston's in Staffordshire. Their brother Herbert was in
Madrid with his father, and Constantia wrote to tell him of
the visit.

> That you may see how Mr Fanshawe has spent his time
> here I have sent you these verses, which are of his making
> since his coming hither ; and he presented them to my
> sister and me. The first were made upon this occasion :
> we were all walking in the old hall, and looking upon
> Trent, and I was speaking how you used to course your
> dog† Dick about that meadow, and talking of many things.
> But the next morning he came out with these verses.

These were the sonnet called *A Dream*, in which, following
Spenser's *Prothalamion*, Fanshawe compliments the Aston
sisters as two swans coming proudly down the stream of
Trent. Constantia gaily tells her brother, 'we made him
believe that you should fight with him when he came into

---

* These lines seem to have been suggested by a sonnet of Bartolome
Leonardo de Argensola, which Fanshawe translated.

† In *Tixall Poetry* where the letter is printed the text reads 'boy' ; but
this must surely be a misreading of Constantia's handwriting.

Spain again, for abusing your sisters so in flattering them so infinitely as he has done in these verses'.

She goes on to tell of the occasion of the other verses which she was enclosing, 'which are made in particular to my sister Gatt' (Gertrude).

> We had been one evening at bowls, and when we came in my sister was opening her hair with her fingers, and bid him tell you that she would not curl her hair no otherwise than it curled itself till she saw you again.

The gallant Richard thereupon composed his lines *On a Lady that vowed not to curl her hair till her brother returned from beyond sea*, in which he pays her delightful compliment. Because she is fair her hair cannot mourn her brother's absence in black, but must be allowed to droop in neglect. But the tresses need no art, for Nature is their mistress, and now they

> *So wind themselves in wreaths, and curl now more*
> *By carelessness than by her care before.*

Finally Gertrude's determination to languish in her brother's absence cannot succeed, for

> *Lady, what boots neglect of face or hair?*
> *You must use art if you will grow less fair.*

These verses were among those which Arthur Clifford found in a trunk at Tixall, Lord Aston's principal seat, and in 1813 he printed them in his volume of *Tixall Poetry*.

Such then was the delightful society in which the young Richard Fanshawe wrote his earliest poems : a society which expected verse to grace its intimate occasions and to comment on public events. This poem to Gertrude Aston is the last in the manuscript now in the British Museum, most of it in Fanshawe's own hand, which he may have left in England on his return to Madrid later in the year.

The Spenserian influence apparent in *A Dream* is equally marked in the longest poem he had yet written, *A Canto of the Progress of Learning*. Two versions of this are to be found in his manuscript book, both in Spenserian stanzas, and the final version begins with a twofold invocation to the Muse and to Spenser's ghost. The *Mutability Cantos* of *The Faerie Queene* are the particular model for Fanshawe's *Canto*, which describes a contest between Wit, defined as 'the use of Reason', and Craft, which is a counterfeit of Wit, to determine

To whom the world pertains most rightfully.

Judgment is given by Nature to Craft, and Wit discomfited mounts on an eagle to fly towards the heavens. The poem is a rather crude allegory touching on the contrast between the world of contemplation and the world of action, with the conclusion that in the latter Craft is the more likely to succeed. Such cynicism seems youthful, and is not in keeping with Fanshawe's mature character as we know it from Lady Fanshawe's *Memoirs*. In the manuscript the poem precedes those to the Aston sisters and was presumably written before them, at the time of his first contact with the political world as an unpaid attaché in Madrid. It is notable principally for the ease with which he uses the Spenserian stanza, which he was the first of a long and distinguished line of poets to adopt. Spenser's immediate successors, Daniel and Drayton, had kept to the older and thoroughly tried rhyme royal or *ottava rima*; Giles and Phineas Fletcher experimented with not very successful variants, without venturing on Spenser's stanza itself. But Fanshawe's accurate ear enabled him to use Spenser's music for a Spenserian allegory, and the experiment proved valuable when, a few years later, he came to translate Virgil.

Fanshawe was back in England again in May 1637 when he saw *The Sovereign of the Seas* on the stocks at Woolwich. This famous ship was then one of the sights of London, but she was still unnamed, for she was not launched until 13 October. Fanshawe addresses her as 'Escorial of the Sea' and proposes as her name *The Charlemagne*, or *The Edgar*

> *to revive his memory*
> *Who so long since o'er land and ocean reigned.*

This must have seemed a likely suggestion for the ship's figure-head was carved to represent King Edgar. Fanshawe imagines her launching, for which Neptune is impatient :

> *Behold she comes, decked like a royal maid !*
> *Her anchors are tucked up, her flags displayed,*
> *Which fan the air, and offer in a scorn*
> *Waves to the river, purple to the morn.*
> *Her chaste white sail is borne up by the wind*
> *Which, like a nimble page, waits close behind.*
> *She mixing her much beauty with due state*
> *Moves soberly with a majestic gait,*
> *And o'er the crystal stream, her lord to please,*
> *A thousand graceful gestures practises.*

Fanshawe printed with this poem, as with the poem on the Escorial, a translation into Latin hexameters. Earlier versions of several of the English lines survive in manuscript and from these we can deduce that the English poems were written first, for the Latin translates the final versions. Fanshawe was a good Latinist, as Pepys records : he approached Fanshawe when his master, Sir Edward Montagu, was to be ennobled in 1660, to draw up the preamble to the patent of nobility. Fanshawe had done the same for General Monck very well, so the Attorney-General * told Pepys, and he made a fitting record of Montagu's services to Charles II. His translation into Latin of John Fletcher's *The Faithful Shepherdess*, however much we may think it supererogatory, also shows his mastery of Latin.

Fanshawe returned from Spain in 1638 to an England already darkening with the shadows of coming rebellion. By April 1640 he was Secretary to the Council of War in Ireland, under the Earls of Strafford and Ormonde. Strafford himself had left Ireland some months before but Fanshawe's friendship with his son must date from this time. The next poem of his which can be dated was occasioned by the humiliating disgrace of Strafford's trial and execution in the spring of 1641. In it Fanshawe is concerned only with the Roman stoicism of Strafford's behaviour :

Thus had great Julius spoke, and looked.

He had not yet the experience to measure the catastrophe to King Charles as could Archbishop Laud, himself awaiting in the Tower the same fate. 'He knew not how to be, or to be made, great', Laud truly wrote of the King. Fanshawe's loyalty was unquestioning, and so it remained.

He was back in England later in the summer of 1641, and succeeded his eldest brother as King's Remembrancer. Early in 1643 he joined the King at Oxford, and about a year later he entered the service of the Prince of Wales as Secretary of War. On 18 May 1644, shortly after receiving this appointment, he married Ann Harrison, a distant cousin, at Wolvercote Church. The marriage was one of utmost felicity, as we may see in the *Memoirs* which Lady Fanshawe wrote when she had been ten years a widow — the most charming record

* Sir Geoffrey Palmer. He had been a witness at Fanshawe's marriage.

of a happy marriage in English, made all the more moving because of her response to the alarms and separations which they had to endure during the Civil War. But, so far as we know, Richard Fanshawe addressed no poems to her and made no poetic record of their happiness; indeed the only original poems written after his marriage which survive are two addressed to the Prince of Wales, 'at his going into the West' in March 1645, and 'in the West' early in 1646. Even this latter poem is a paraphrase of a Latin poem by George Buchanan to James VI, and from this time on Fanshawe devoted his gifts entirely to those translations which are his greatest achievement.

We may suppose that from time to time he went on with his translations from Horace which he had begun early in his life — twenty are to be found in the manuscript which (I have suggested) ends in 1636 — until he was ready to publish them in 1652. There had also been the translations from Martial and Boethius before ever he went abroad, and in Spain he had translated a number of sonnets by Luís de Góngora and Bartolomé Leonardo de Argensola. The more sustained task of translating from the *Aeneid* he perhaps undertook after his return to England but before he was caught up in the catastrophe of Civil War. At least this seems the most probable date, for the Spenserian stanzas which he used for his version of the fourth book, *On the Loves of Dido and Aeneas*, are likely to have followed not long after his experiment with the form in *The Progress of Learning*. He had there shown his understanding of Spenser's apt and varied rhythms, and in employing the stanza for translating from the *Aeneid* he demonstrated how well he understood both the complexity of his task and Spenser's metrical intention.

Spenser's bold creation of a new form of verse for the poem which won him the title of the English Virgil, to which, as *The Shepheardes Calendar* shows, he had long aspired, was an attempt to match in English the qualities of Virgil's prosody. He prefaced *The Faerie Queene* with a paraphrase of the lines (then thought to be by Virgil himself) which traditionally introduced the *Aeneid*, alluding in these, as Virgil was believed to have done, to his earlier pastorals. He intended his readers, no less than Milton after him, to remember Virgil as they read. Milton, also wishing to get the effect of Virgil's metre, used blank verse as Surrey had done ; but Spenser's adaptation of the *ottava rima* in which Ariosto and Tasso had written their epics was more subtly designed to draw out the sense from one verse to another. For whereas the eight-line Italian stanza naturally falls into two parts (six lines cross-rhymed and then a rhymed couplet) Spenser's stanza continues the rhythm through nine rhyme-linked lines, and while permitting division at any point, even in the middle of a line, does not compel division anywhere. Again, in the Italian stanza the final couplet is conclusive, often epigrammatic, but the lengthening of the last line in Spenser's stanza prevents these effects and leads the ear on to the succeeding stanza, so that a poem in Spenserian stanzas is not broken up into separate units but is built up into a long, continuous rhythm. By his invention therefore Spenser achieved the result which Milton strove for in blank verse while at the same time maintaining the grace and smoothness of Virgil. He could, like Virgil or Milton, prolong the rhythmical impulse beyond the reader's expectation with majestic effect ; he could also insert lyrical passages into his narrative without awkwardness, as Milton seldom succeeded in doing. Where Milton is most successful in this, in Eve's speech to Adam in Book IV of *Paradise Lost*,

With thee conversing I forget all time,

he devises a repetition of her positive statement 'With thee
. . .' in the negative 'Without thee . . .'. It is done with con-
summate skill, but the resulting passage is stanzaic in sound,
and of such a nature that it could not often be repeated in a
poem in blank verse without seeming mannered. Spenser
could do this whenever he wished and through his stanza
came closer than Surrey or Milton or Dryden to achieving
the complexity of overall rhythm together with the smoothness within the line which characterizes the *Aeneid*. Fanshawe's choice of his stanza for translating Book IV therefore
showed the insight of a metrist of genius who, as his translations from Horace had already proved, was eager to discover
the best way of transposing into English accentual verse the
alien forms of classical prosody.

He manages the Spenserian stanza with fine assurance, as
in the contrast between Dido's frantic speech to Aeneas on
discovering his intention to sail away and Aeneas's calm
reply.

> *Didst thou hope too by stealth to leave my land,*
> *And that such treason could be unbetrayed?*
> *Nor should my love, nor thy late plighted hand,*
> *Nor Dido, who would die, thy flight have stayed?*
> *Must too this voyage be in winter made?*
> *— Through storms? O cruel to thyself and me!*
> *Didst thou not hunt strange lands, and sceptres swayed*
> *By others? If old Troy revived should be,*
> *Should Troy itself be sought through a tempestuous sea?*

And Aeneas 'thus in short replied' :

> *For me, O Queen, I never will deny*
> *But that I owe you more than you can say,*
> *Nor shall I stick to bear in memory*
> *Eliza's name, whilst memory doth stay*

> *In this frail seat, whilst breath these limbs doth sway.*
> *But to the point. I never did intend*
> *(Pray charge me not with that) to steal away ;*
> *And much less did I wedlock-bands pretend,*
> *Neither to such a treaty ever condescend.*

Fanshawe uses the rhythms within the stanza, as Spenser would have done, to contrast the brusque brutality of Aeneas with the desperate misery of Dido, his determination with her helplessness. J. W. Mackail said of Fanshawe's translation that 'for combined dignity and sweetness it is unsurpassed by what any other rendering of Virgil into English has achieved'. There is no need to dissent from the judgment of a great Virgilian scholar.

One more translation Fanshawe undertook during the time of civil war, about 1643 or 1644, Guarini's famous pastoral play *Il pastor fido*. He had never been in Italy, but his knowledge of the language must have been profound, for Guarini's style is one of ingenious and elaborate refinement, which could easily be missed or spoilt in translation, as it had been in the crude Dymock version published in 1602. Fanshawe's translation very well represents Guarini's manner, though without attempting a literal rendering. He produces something acceptable to his own generation of Englishmen, instead of attempting the absurd task of showing in English what Guarini meant to sixteenth-century Italians. He disregards Guarini's preferences among the rhetorical figures because they were no longer in fashion ; and for the unrhymed hendecasyllables and heptasyllables of the Italian he substitutes decasyllabic or octosyllabic couplets. In this he was following the precedent of English pastoral drama in *The Faithful Shepherdess*, which would be familiar to English readers, instead of puzzling them with an alien convention.

Sir John Denham, who also had been with the King in Oxford in 1643–1644, wrote a commendatory poem in which he remarked the new qualities of Fanshawe's method in translation, which differed strongly from Jonson's literalness.

> That servile path thou nobly dost decline
> Of tracing word by word and line by line :
> Those are the laboured births of slavish brains,
> Not the effects of poetry, but pains,
> Cheap vulgar arts, whose narrowness affords
> No flight for thoughts, but poorly sticks at words.
> A new and nobler way thou dost pursue
> To make translations and translators too.
> They but preserve the ashes, thou the flame,
> True to his sense, but truer to his fame,
> Fording his current where thou find'st it low,
> Lett'st in thine own to make it rise and flow,
> Wisely restoring whatsoever grace
> It lost by change of times, or tongues, or place ;
> Nor fettered to his numbers and his times
> Betray'st his music to unhappy rhymes ;
> Nor are the nerves of his compacted strength
> Stretched and dissolved into unsinewed length ;
> Yet after all (lest we should think it thine)
> Thy spirit to his circle dost confine.

This perceptive criticism by a fellow-poet may be applied to all Fanshawe's translations. He never attempted the banal literalness of line by line. He accepted the challenge of finding an appropriate (but usually dissimilar) metrical form. He skilfully solved the problem, which besets all who translate from the more highly inflected Romance languages into the comparatively uninflected English, of allowing their compacted strength to be stretched and dissolved among the

Sir Richard Fanshawe

inevitably increased number of words required. And he was constantly successful in the translator's paramount task of restoring to the work translated

> *whatsoever grace*
> *It lost by change of times, or tongues, or place,*

being aware that change of times and place were no less important than change of tongues.

Guarini's tragi-comedy, which so much affected literary taste in the century after its production, long since lost its appeal : for us it has at best the charm of a period piece, and Fanshawe's translation must suffer with it. Yet this is often so felicitous that we can easily understand how *Il pastor fido* once enjoyed such fame. In the third act Corisca, alone with Amaryllis, for her own malicious purposes tries to persuade her to the philosophy of 'Gather ye rose-buds while ye may'.

> *But when our youth and beauty (which alone*
> *Conquers the strength and wit of men) are gone,*
> *All's gone with us ; nor canst thou possibly*
> *Say a worse thing, or to be pardoned thee*
> *More hardly, than 'Old woman'. Then before*
> *Thou split on that inevitable shore,*
> *Know thine own worth, and do not be so mad,*
> *As when thou mayst live merry, to live sad.*
> *What would the lion's strength boot him, or wit*
> *Avail a man, unless he used it ?*
> *Our beauty is to us that which to men*
> *Wit is, or strength unto the lion. Then*
> *Let us use it whilst we may ;*
> *Snatch those joys that haste away.*
> *Earth her winter-coat may cast*
> *And renew her beauty past ;*

But, our winter come, in vain
We solicit spring again :
And when our furrows snow shall cover
Love may return, but never lover.

Guarini acknowledged his debt to Catullus for those last lines, but to his translation of them Fanshawe brought other enriching memories, of Fletcher, and of Shakespeare. Thus he naturalized *Il pastor fido* in English, and made it read like an English play rather than as a Mediterranean pastoral shivering in our cold climate.

In 1647 Fanshawe published, as his first book, this translation of *Il pastor fido* with a dedication to the Prince of Wales in which he made application (as it was then termed) of the plot of Guarini's play to the unhappy condition of England. 'Because it seems to me a landscape of these kingdoms, (your royal patrimony,) as well in the former flourishing, as in the present distractions thereof, I thought it not improper for your princely notice at this time.' In the following year the book was re-issued with the addition of Fanshawe's original poems and his translation of *Aeneid* IV. There were further editions in 1664, 1676, and 1692, the last being merely a reprint of the edition of 1676. In 1677 Elkanah Settle slightly adapted the play, without acknowledgment, for presentation at the Duke's Theatre. In 1726 Fanshawe's translation with the Italian text on facing pages was printed again. It was the most successful of his published works, in testimony to the contemporary fame of Guarini's play. We should be foolish therefore to blame Fanshawe for wasting so rare a gift as a translator on a work which we no longer esteem as did his contemporaries ; he was writing for them. Besides, it might not be an easy task to prove their taste inferior to our own.

During the next few years the Fanshawes shared the distresses and dangers of all loyal subjects of King Charles. They were with the King at Hampton Court in 1647, and after his flight from there they went over to France. Lady Fanshawe records on this occasion an incident which is very revealing of her husband's English sang-froid. They were walking by the seaside when 'two ships of the Dutch, then in war with England, shot bullets at us, so near that we heard them whizz by us ; at which I called to my husband to make haste back, and began to run. But he altered not his pace, saying, If we must be killed it were as good to be killed walking as running.' During the next few years they travelled about on the Prince's business between London and Paris, Holland and Ireland, Spain and Scotland, sometimes together, often separated, loyally encountering discomfort and disaster in every shape from Dutch bullets and Turkish pirates to Irish ghosts and fleas, until in September 1651 Sir Richard * was taken prisoner at the Battle of Worcester and brought to Whitehall. There Lady Fanshawe went every night ' when the clock struck four in the morning, with a dark lantern in my hand, all alone and on foot. . . . There I would go under his window and softly call him. He that after the first time expected me, never failed to put out his head at the first call. Thus we talked together ; and sometimes I was so wet with rain that it went in at my neck and out at my heels.' After about ten weeks he was released through the good offices of his family doctor, who happened also to be Cromwell's, for he was sick of the scurvy.

In 1652 he brought together and published the translations from Horace which he had been making for twenty years or more. These were reprinted in the collection of translations of all Horace's poems which Alexander Brome

* He was made baronet in September 1650.

edited in 1666. They show, no less than his translations
from Virgil and Guarini, his exceptional sensitivity to poetry
in other languages, and his virtuosity as a translator. In all
he translated forty-five of the Odes (but one he chose not to
print) and seven of the Epodes, a little less than half the total.
Among the most famous is the second Ode of the fourth
book,

Pindarum quisquis studet aemulari,

in which Horace gives warning against attempts at rivalling
the poets of Greece.

> *Who thinks to equal Pindar, tries*
> *With waxen wings to reach the skies,*
> *Like him that (falling) a name gave*
>   *To his watery grave.*
>
> *As a proud stream that swollen with rain*
> *Comes pouring down the hills amain,*
> *So Pindar flows, and fears no drouth,*
>   *Such his deep mouth,*
>
> *Worthy the bays, whether he pour*
> *From unexhausted springs a shower*
> *Of lawless dithyrambs, and thunders*
>   *In bolder numbers :*
>
> *Or sings of Gods and Heroes, etc.*

He maintains Horace's image, and represents the onward
rush of the Sapphics with his own stanza ; and he preserves
the compacted strength of the lines, which is a harder task
with Horace than with Guarini.

He can respond equally well to the light-hearted gaiety of
a poem such as the sixteenth Ode of the third book, in which

Horace, writing to Maecenas, notes that though everything gives way to gold, he is content with his humbler lot.

> *With growing riches cares augment,*
> *And thirst of greater. I did well*
> *To shrink my head into my shell,*
> *Maecenas, knighthood's ornament.*
>
> *The more a man to himself denies,*
> *The more indulgent Heaven bestows.*
> *I'm with the party of the Noes :*
> *Let them that will side with the Ayes.**

Here he is using the stanza long afterwards made famous through *In Memoriam*, which Ben Jonson and Lord Herbert had recently used, but more often he uses his own adaptation to represent Horace's favourite Alcaic stanza, as in the third Ode of the second book, which must have seemed especially relevant to Fanshawe in the 1640s,

> *Aequam memento rebus in arduis ;*

or better still in the yet more famous *Eheu fugaces.*

> *Ah Posthumus ! the years of man*
> *Slide on with winged pace, nor can*
>   *Virtue reprieve her friend*
>   *From wrinkles, age, and end. . . .*
>
> *Thou must forgo thy lands and goods*
> *And pleasing wife ; nor of thy woods*
>   *Shall any follow thee*
>   *But the sad cypress-tree.*

* In the texts these lines are printed in the reverse order, Ayes before Noes ; but the stanza requires that they should be arranged as I have ventured to print them.

Thy worthy heir shall then carouse
Thy hoarded wines, and wash the house
With better sack than that
Which makes the abbots fat.

(These last lines provide a good example of Fanshawe's regard for change of times, which Denham noted.) At his best in these translations Fanshawe achieves that extraordinary combination of highly wrought artistry with colloquial diction which characterizes Horace's Odes. And in temperament he was very close to Horace : calm, gentle, humorous, detached, or, as Lady Fanshawe describes him, 'very obliging to all, and forward to serve his master, his country and friends, cheerful in his conversation. . . . I never heard him hold dispute in my life, but he would often speak against it, saying it was an uncharitable custom, which never returned to the advantage of either party. . . . And so free from passion that made him beloved of all who knew him.' In a note to the seventh Ode of Book IV Fanshawe shows his admiration for Horace's true Epicureanism, which is not a mere sensual hedonism, but a sensible preference for tranquillity of mind and body, and a liking for sober reason 'that sifts into the causes of things, why any thing is to be chosen or declined ; and avoiding those controversial disputes by which minds are (for the most part) rapt farther into error and engaged in animosities'. Thus he imputed to Horace those very qualities which his wife discerned in him ; and this sympathy made him as good an interpreter as Horace has yet found in English.

In the winter of 1653 he took a lease of Tankersley Park in Yorkshire from the Earl of Strafford, and while living there 'an innocent country life, minding only the country sports and the country affairs', he undertook the largest and

most exacting of all his translations, *Os Lusiadas* of Luis de
Camoens. For his other translations he had had English
predecessors more often than not, and, though he had no
need of their assistance for his understanding, they offered a
challenge which he was glad to accept. He had written not
the first but the best translation of the fourth book of the
Aeneid, of Horace's Odes, of *Il pastor fido* ; now he accepted
a different challenge, to present for the first time to English
readers (few of whom, we may suppose, had any knowledge
of Portuguese), the national epic of Portugal, which Tasso
himself had regarded as a rival to *Gerusalemme liberata*.

There are good reasons for thinking that *The Lusiad* is a
first draft, published prematurely without Fanshawe's authority. The editor of his correspondence in the eighteenth century said that this was so, and that it had been printed before
'he could put his last finishing strokes' to it.* Internal evidence confirms this, and, as we can see from the manuscript
of his early poems, Fanshawe worked over his poems carefully, revising and recasting as he thought desirable. There
are some unmetrical lines left in *The Lusiad*, which would
hardly have been acceptable to so accurate an ear as his ; and
the title suggests ignorance of the Portuguese language (which
can hardly have been his) since *Os Lusiadas* means 'the sons
of Lusus' and is not analogous to the *Iliad* or the *Aeneid*.
(The running title, *The Luciad*, is still more ridiculous, and
even if Fanshawe intended publication in 1655, as the date
on his dedication implies, he cannot have read the proofs.)
Thus his translation lacks the polish and distinction which he
gave to *Il pastor fido* and is sometimes clumsy or inept ; this
is unfortunate, for Camoens is one of the great poets of Renaissance Europe, and Guarini is not.

* This may derive from an inattentive reading of Fanshawe's Post-
script to the translation from Petronius which precedes *The Lusiad*.

Whether or not *The Lusiad* was an unfinished draft, it was
a remarkable feat to translate a poem of nearly nine thousand
lines in at most sixteen months. (As Fanshawe told Lord
Strafford, 'from the hour I began it to the end thereof, I slept
not once out of these walls' of Tankersley Park, to which
they had gone in March 1653, and which they left, so Lady
Fanshawe says, at the end of July 1654.) He used the same
stanza, *oitavas, ottava rima,* as the original, a measure already
established in English for the historical poem by Daniel and
Drayton, and well suited to the narrative of Vasco da Gama's
voyage to the Indies in 1497. Fanshawe cannot match the
lyrical passion of Camoens' verse, but he does convey the
patriotic enthusiasm, and the sense of immediacy which
Camoens, who had himself been in the East and knew the
dangers of the long ocean voyage and of tropical, strange
lands, so vividly presents. And he manages admirably the
contrast, at the end of Canto IV, between the bustle and
excitement of setting out on the great voyage and the oracular
pessimism of the Old Man of Restelo, who, at the very
instant when Vasco da Gama is about to sail, derides the
pursuit of Honour which is the motive of every man taking
part.

> *Now in the famous port of Lisbon town*
> *(Where golden Tagus mingles his sweet flood*
> *With the salt Ocean, and his sands doth drown),*
> *With noble longings and transported mood*
> *The ships lie ready. There no sullen frown,*
> *No frosty fear, benumbs the youthful blood :*
> > *For both the seamen and the land-men there*
> > *Will go with me about the world, they swear.*
>
> *Upon the shore the strutting soldiers sail*
> *In clothes of several colour, several cut,*

Their minds more brave, bent to extend our pale,
And plant in lands unknown their daring foot.
The gentle wind breathing a tempting gale,
On the tall ships the standards ope and shut.
  The ships expect, for this new navigation,
  To be (like Argo) made a constellation.

Then the old man raises his voice, which 'rattled in our shrouds', and speaks to them all.

O glory of commanding ! O vain thirst
Of that same empty nothing we call Fame !
O Ignis fatuus, kindled and nursed
With vulgar breath — and this we Honour name !
What plagues, what stings, what secret scourges cursed
Torment those bosoms which thou dost inflame !
  What deaths ! what dangers ! what impetuous
    storms !
  What cruelties on them thy hand performs !

Fell tyrant of the souls ! Life's swallowing wave !
Mother of plunders and black rapes unchaste !
The secret miner, and the open grave
Of patrimonies, kingdoms, empires vast !
They call thee noble, and they call thee brave
— Worthy to have other names upon thee cast !
  They call thee Fame, and Glory sovereign :
  Titles with which the foolish rout is ta'en. . . .

Accursed be he who first forsook the ground
And fastened canvas wings to a dry tree !
Worthy in endless darkness to be bound
If that which I was taught religion be.
May never judgment solid and profound,
May never happy vein in poetry

Retrieve his memory, adorn his fame,
But die with him his glory and his name.

This extraordinary episode invites Fanshawe's most sensitive response, just because it is so unexpected in a patriotic heroic poem to find the whole basis of such action questioned.

Camoens' poetry is as Portuguese as Manueline architecture, and derives from the same source. The Portuguese are a Latin people who have turned their backs on the Mediterranean, and at the Renaissance they drew their inspiration not from the rediscovered world of classical antiquity but from the newly discovered world of their own voyages. In the carved doorways and windows of these buildings is none of the smooth, cool elegance of marble but instead the rough feel of sea-splashed rope or of timbers encrusted with barnacles. So too Camoens, for all his debt to Virgil and his constant comparison of Portuguese and Roman, owes more to his own experience of the sea-route to India, so that his poem, like Manueline architecture, is very unlike anything else in Europe. This exotic quality recurs again and again, and is by Fanshawe perhaps best suggested in the description of the giant Adamastor, the guardian of the Cape of Good Hope.

His thick bush-beard and his long hair (which hung
Dangling upon his shoulders from his head)
Were spongy weeds, so wet they might be wrung,
Which never comb seemed to have harrowed.
The nitty points thereof were tagged, were strung
With dark blue mussels, of their own filth bred.
He had (for a montera *) on his crown
The shell of a red lobster overgrown.

* A hunter's cap, round, with ear-flaps.

His body naked, and his genitals,
That he might swim with greater speed and ease :
But with maritime little animals
By hundreds covered and all hid were these,
As crayfish, shrimps, and other fish that crawls
(Receiving theirs from the pale moon's increase),
Oysters, and periwinkles with their slime,
Snails, with their houses on their backs that climb.

Roy Campbell, who in our own day showed himself as versatile a translator as Fanshawe, might have made the best of all translations of *Os Lusiadas*, for his translation of Camoens' Canção IX is a masterpiece. But (so far as I know) he translated only a few lines from Canto VII, and those into heroic couplets, and we must be content with Fanshawe for the most spirited version in English, however far it falls short of the noble original.

His next task was a translation from the Spanish of Antonio Hurtado de Mendoza of his masque *Querer por solo querer*, which he dedicated in July 1654 to Queen Christina of Sweden. For some reason this, together with a version of the same poet's *Fiestas de Aranjuez* remained unpublished until after his death. In 1648 he had published translations of ten sonnets from the Spanish of Luís de Góngora and Bartolomé Leonardo de Argensola, and nine more by the same poets have recently been printed. For all but two of these sonnets he uses the form which Surrey had established in English. The best known is his version of Góngora's *Vana rosa*.

> *Blown in the morning, thou shalt fade ere noon :*
> *What boots a life which in such haste forsakes thee ?*
> *Thou art wondrous frolic being to die so soon,*
> *And passing proud a little colour makes thee.*

If thee thy brittle beauty so deceives,
Know then the thing that swells thee is thy bane ;
For the same beauty doth in bloody leaves
The sentence of thy early death contain.
Some clown's coarse lungs will poison thy sweet flower
If by the careless plough thou shalt be torn ;
And many Herods lie in wait each hour
To murder thee as soon as thou art born,
*   Nay, force thy bud to blow, their tyrant breath*
*   Anticipating life to hasten death.*

Clearly Fanshawe was well-read in the sonnets of the
1590s to make a sonnet which reads as if it were native
English.

In 1658 he published the last of his work to appear in his
lifetime, the Latin version of *The Faithful Shepherdess*. Thereafter he became too much engaged in public affairs to have
time for writing. In September of that year Cromwell died,
and three weeks later Fanshawe obtained leave to go abroad,
where he joined King Charles in Paris. His devoted wife
contrived, by means of forging a passport, to join him, and in
1660 they returned to England with the King. Fanshawe
became Secretary of the Latin Tongue, and may have helped
to prevent molestation of his predecessor in that office, John
Milton. In 1661 he escorted Catherine of Braganza from
Portugal to England. The remaining years of his life he
spent mostly in Portugal or Spain, to each of which he was
sent Ambassador, and he died suddenly in Madrid in June
1666, just as he was preparing to return to England.

Lady Fanshawe, after recording his death in the *Memoirs*
which she wrote for their son ten years later, quoted here
from his translation of the ninth Ode of the fourth book of
Horace.

Lollio, thou art a man has skill
To fathom things ; that being tried
In either fortune couldst abide
In both upright ; and Lollio still.
Of covetous fraud a scourge severe,
On whom the all-attracting gold
Could with his tenters ne'er take hold ;
Nor consul of one year. Whene'er
A virtuous magistrate and true
Shall call good gain, bid bribes avaunt,
Upon opposers' bellies plant
His conquering flags, — Lollio, that's you.
He is not happy who hath much ;
But whoso can his mind dispose
To use aright what Heaven bestows,
He justly is accounted such ;
If he know how hard want to bear,
And fears a crime more than his end,
If, for his country or his friend,
To stake his life he do not fear.

Lady Fanshawe's judgment of its aptness cannot be questioned, and we may suppose that Sir Richard would have wished for no better epitaph than these words of his beloved Horace, 'Prince of Lyrics, and of all Latin poets the fullest fraught with excellent morality', the poet whose company he had kept longest of all those whom he had made English.

TEXTS

There is no complete edition of Sir Richard Fanshawe's works, but the following have been published recently :

The Lusiad of Luis de Camoens, ed. J. D. M. Ford, Cambridge, Mass.,
Harvard University Press, 1940.

Il pastor fido, ed. W. F. Staton and W. E. Simeone, Oxford, Clarendon Press, 1964.

Shorter Poems and Translations, ed. N. W. Bawcutt, Liverpool University Press, 1964 (reprints the poems added to *Il pastor fido* in 1648, including the translation of *Aeneid* IV, and some additional poems).

7

CHARLES COTTON

CHARLES COTTON is remembered now, and will always be remembered for his share in the most popular book in the English language. The second part which he added to his friend Izaak Walton's *Compleat Angler* in 1676 is altogether in keeping with the first part, which Walton had published more than twenty years before. His description of the austerer country of the High Peak, bright with its clear rivers, fills out the portrayal of rural England that Walton, by the slow and gentle chalk-streams of Hampshire, had originally created. That, surely, is the source of the endless delight English people have found in their book : it showed the face of England as we like to think of it, and invented the image of an English summer day in the country. Walton and Cotton intended most of all to be practical, to instruct their fellows 'how to angle for a Trout or Grayling in a clear stream'. But angling is the recreation of a contemplative man, of a man who has time to stand and stare, who enjoys the whistle and flash of a kingfisher over his stream, the rustle of leaves in alder and poplar, the play of light dappling the rough willow trunks, the smell of mown hay in neighbouring fields, the glimpse, here and there above the trees, of limestone rock and russet moor.

Walton confessed to his readers that the book was also a picture of his own disposition, not only a portrait of the quiet English countryside, therefore, but a self-portrait also.

When he invited Charles Cotton to add a discourse on fly-
fishing, he must have been very confident in his judgment of
him both as a man and as an angler ; surprisingly so, when
we remember the difference of thirty-seven years between
them, and the social chasm separating the London iron-
monger and the country gentleman. But a common interest
in literature and in fishing enabled them to enjoy a happy and
unaffected friendship, as we may see in the charming letter of
acknowledgment which Walton printed after Cotton's discourse, and in the poems which Cotton addressed to him on
various occasions. One of these poems, *The Retirement*,
which Cotton had sent to Walton some years before,
Walton now ventured to print at the close of their book,
because it would give their readers 'a good picture of both ;
and so much of your own mind too, as will make any reader
that is blessed with a generous soul to love you the better'.

I

Farewell thou busy world, and may
  We never meet again.
Here I can eat, and sleep, and pray,
And do more good in one short day,
  Than he who his whole age outwears
Upon the most conspicuous theatres,
Where nought but vice and vanity do reign.

II

Good God ! how sweet are all things here !
How beautiful the fields appear !
How cleanly do we feed and lie !
Lord ! what good hours do we keep !
  How quietly we sleep !
What peace, what unanimity !

Charles Cotton

How innocent from the lewd fashion
Is all our business, all our conversation !

'Here' is Cotton's home by the river Dove, where two years
before he had built the little Fishing-House, a sort of temple
dedicated to the river and its sportsmen, *Piscatoribus sacrum* ;
over the door, twisted together in monogram, he had carved
his own and his old friend's initials.

VI

Oh my beloved nymph ! fair Dove,
Princess of rivers, how I love
Upon thy flowery banks to lie,
And view thy silver stream,
When gilded by a summer's beam !
And in it all thy wanton fry
Playing at liberty,
And with my angle upon them
The all of treachery
I ever learned, to practise and to try !

The poem, as Walton says, tells us much of Cotton. Indeed
he regularly reveals far more of himself than do most writers
of his time in his poetry : perhaps that is one reason for
Wordsworth's and Coleridge's and Charles Lamb's vivid
enjoyment of it.

The hint of nostalgia in this poem, as throughout *The
Compleat Angler*, derives not from the hankering of a towns-
man but from the contrast between the peace of the countryside observed by a countryman and the political and other
troubles of a busy world. For the countryside that Cotton
describes is known intimately, as by one who was born and
bred there ; it is a place not of refuge, but of active pleasure,
not for holidays but for every day, a place from which
reluctant, necessary excursions may be made to the city.

Here the infinite consequence of the shifting seasons is
realized ; rain, wind, and sun have their elaborate, indirect
part in man's life through soil, and crops, and cattle. The
river Dove is a source of pleasure to Cotton not alone for its
sound and sparkle, and for the fanciful limestone rocks in
the dale, but because (having discovered every yard of it
himself in the absorbed and stealthy explorations of childhood) he knew the secret caves where he could smile as he
hid from his creditors, and because he knew which pools
would offer himself and his friends best sport. So the
delightful river dances through Cotton's poems, suggesting
always the deep affection he had for his own countryside.

By the river Dove, at Beresford Hall, Charles Cotton was
born in the spring of 1630, probably on 28 April. There,
apart from brief visits to London and travels to France and
to Ireland, he was to live all his life. He was aware of his
good fortune and would never have provoked the Horatian
rebuke : *O nimium fortunatos bona si sua norint*. I suppose
nothing — no ambition, no offer of place or reward — would
have persuaded him to live anywhere else. He was bred to
be a country gentleman, to play his part in the life of his own
house, of his own place and people. He did not, as so many
nowadays, merely sleep and spend the week-ends in the
country : he lived and worked there, was of a piece with the
life about him, not an amused spectator of it uncertainly relying on the instruction of books. The High Peak was to him
not romantically picturesque, not a National Park to be
preserved for the recreation of town-dwellers ; it was his
home, and, for all his observations upon its harsh weather and
rough folk, he loved it. So, when Viator comes down in the
morning after his arrival at Beresford Hall and says that he
now thinks it 'a marvellous pretty place', Cotton tells him,
'whether you think so or no, you cannot oblige me more

than to say so ; and those of my friends who know my humour, and are so kind as to comply with it, usually flatter me that way'.

Whenever he had to go away — he never went away of his own choice — he felt lost and homesick ; and he hurried back to Beresford Hall as soon as he could, as we see him in the opening pages of his part of *The Compleat Angler*. He much preferred to entertain his friends there rather than to visit them in London, and we can be certain that he entertained them generously, with good sport in the day and afterwards with good food and drink and good talk. First and foremost he was, as he said, 'an old-fashioned country squire', and from this come all his original writings. *The Compleat Angler* ; *The Compleat Gamester* (or, Instructions how to play at Billiards, Trucks, Bowls, and Chess. Together with all manner of usual and most Gentle Games, either on Cards, or Dice. To which is added, the Acts and Mysteries of Riding, Racing, Archery, and Cock-fighting) ; *The Planters Manual* (Being Instructions for the Raising, Planting, and Cultivating all sorts of Fruit-Trees, whether Stone-fruits or Pepin-fruits, with their Natures and Seasons. Very useful for such as are Curious in Planting and Grafting) — these are the sort of books a lively and public-spirited country gentleman might write in any age. But the poems too come from the same source, from Cotton's wish to share with his fellows his knowledge and love of the English countryside and its ways, especially of his own countryside. For if we are born in the country then all our life such words as river, hill, valley, wood, hedge, wall, roof, will retain local connotations, which must differentiate Northerner and Southerner, East Anglian and man of the West Country. A hill may bring to one the recollection of heather in September, and the voice of curlew and grouse, but to another of sheep-cropped downland embroidered with summer flowers. Walls may mean angular chunks of white limestone precariously balanced, or thin slabs of grey oolite in carefully laid courses, or smooth cob with thatched tops. And rivers, most evocative of all, may be slow, greenish, silent, meandering through flat, lush meadows; or they may be rapid, direct, flashing white among the rattling stones in their narrow ash-clothed dales. Wordsworth's poetry would have been very different if he had been born and bred in Constable's country, or in Sussex; similarly, Cotton never leaves us in any doubt of his provenance, and (apart from his Virgilian burlesques *) his longest poem describes *The Wonders of the Peake*.

He was born into a family that counted poets among their friends. From his father (also Charles) he would have heard at first hand of Ben Jonson, Donne, Sir Henry Wotton, and John Fletcher, of Henry Glapthorne, and Robert Herrick. Through his father he came to know Sir William Davenant and Richard Lovelace, as well as Walton himself. Perhaps Donne or Wotton had introduced Walton to the elder Cotton, or perhaps it was the other way round. He could hardly have failed to meet Walton who in 1646 married as his second wife Anne, the half-sister of Bishop Ken, for the Bishop had a cottage in Dovedale from which he would have found it difficult, even had he so wished, to exclude his brother-in-law. The elder Cotton was 'a gentleman born to a competent fortune, and so qualified in his person and education, that for many years he continued the greatest ornament of the town, in the esteem of those who had been best bred. . . . He had all those qualities which in youth raise men to the

---

* These poems, which maintained an extraordinary popularity from the 1660s to the early nineteenth century, are scarcely readable now, perhaps because such jazzing of the classics demands a more tenacious recollection of the *Aeneid* than most now enjoy.

reputation of being fine gentlemen ; such a pleasantness and gaiety of humour, such a sweetness and gentleness of nature, and such a civility and delightfulness in conversation, that no man, in the court or out of it, appeared a more accomplished person.' (So Lord Clarendon describes, in his evocative and stylish way, one whom he was pleased to number among his chief acquaintances.) The elder Cotton had built up a good library at Beresford Hall, with among its best treasures a manuscript of *The Mad Lover* which his friend and old companion John Fletcher probably gave him. This he lent at one time to his cousin Sir Aston Cokayne, who was then living mostly at Ashbourne. Cokayne too had many friends among the poets : Donne again, and Drayton upon whom he wrote an elegy ; George Sandys the translator of Ovid's *Metamorphoses*, Tom May the translator of Lucan ; Massinger, Habington, Randolph, and Suckling. The young Charles was thus brought up in a family and in a household where books and learning were an accepted part of a gentleman's equipment, where talk of poets and poetry was as likely to engage them of an evening as talk of farming or of sport or of the bench. In such company he would learn to use the familiar, plain style which Ben Jonson had developed from Horace's epistolary manner, and though he was too young to be one of the sons of Ben, yet certainly he was a grandson, and so learnt, like the rest of the mob of gentlemen, to write with ease.

On his mother's side also he came of distinguished stock. She was Olive, daughter to Sir John Stanhope of Elvaston, who had married the daughter and heiress of Edward Beresford of Beresford. Michael Drayton knew Lady Stanhope and lamented her in an elegy in which he seems to suggest that she had written poems herself. The elder Cotton eloped with Olive Stanhope, then aged fifteen, in 1629. The ensuing altercation with her father ended amicably, but the marriage, begun so romantically, was brought by the husband's extravagance to the eventual indignity of litigation and open dispute. One of Mrs Cotton's letters, written to her steward on 10 May 1650, survives. It is full of instructions about household affairs, and of requests, for the measurements of her bedroom so that she may get fittings for her bed, for two yards of unwrought cushion canvas, for 'a large book in writing with a parchment cover blotched on one side with ink towards the nook of it : it's of preserving and conserving'. She asks about the gardens, 'and tell John gardener that if I do not find my gardens in ampler manner when I come, that he and I shall not be friends'. She sends kindly messages to everyone on the estate, to the old miller and several others by name ; and she signs herself 'Your loving mistress'. She sounds perfectly delightful, and, in spite of the recent troubles with her husband, as gay and vivacious as when 'in her extreme affection' she had run away to marry him.

Charles, their only child, was never so attracted by the great world as his father, and this letter from his mother, much more than Clarendon's portrait of his father, suggests his tastes and temperament. The disastrous times in which he grew up could not have encouraged him to leave the comparative security of Beresford dale, and though he was a convinced and fervent Royalist, by the time he was old enough to take an active part in the King's cause, the cause was lost. One poem, which recalls a famous poem by his friend Richard Lovelace, may imply an intention to take up arms for the King:

> Let the King send me where he please,
> Ready at drum and trumpet's call ;
> I'll fight at home, or cross the seas,
> His soldier, but Chlorinda's thrall.

The most likely date for this seems to be in the summer of 1651, before the Battle of Worcester. His father had preferred the life of the town, among the mob of gentlemen, in the early, happy years of King Charles : to be a man about town during the rule of the Saints can have had fewer attractions than dangers. It was more sensible to wait in patience for the Restoration, reading, learning, fishing, writing poetry, than to challenge the Puritans with irreverent and scurrilous poems, like Tom Weaver, some time Canon of Christ Church, and then find yourself on trial for your life.

Whether Cotton ever had any formal education is not known : it seems probable that for the most part he remained at home, encouraged by his father to read in his library, and to make his first attempts at writing. No less a poet than Herrick acknowledged the critical insight of the elder Cotton, in a poem addressed to him :

> *What state above, what symmetry below,*
> *Lines have, or should have, thou the best canst show.*

He learnt Greek and Latin, Italian and French, and he must have been unusually well read in the English poets and dramatists. There was a number of Italian books at Beresford Hall, as Sir Aston Cokayne tells us, but Cotton's especial interest in foreign literatures was in French, from which, in later years, he made many translations. His father prompted him to the first of these, du Vaix's *Moral Philosophy of the Stoics*, and for his sister-in-law he translated Corneille's *Horace*. The best known of his translations was of Montaigne's *Essays*, which he dedicated to Halifax, who said it was 'the book in the world he was best entertained with'. This may not have achieved the fame of Florio's version, but it has been more constantly read, and deservedly so, since it is much more like Montaigne. But then the calm, retiring English country gentleman had much more in common with Montaigne than had the resolute, irascible Italian lexicographer.

In addition to his father's help, Cotton had as his tutor for a time Ralph Rawson, who had been ejected by the Parliamentary commissioners from his fellowship of Brasenose in 1648. Rawson came from Stockport, in Cheshire, and may have spent some years at Beresford Hall before being admitted at St John's College, Cambridge, in February 1655. To him Cotton dedicated his translation of an ode by Johannes Secundus, to which Rawson replied in verse ; and he introduced Rawson as Thyrsis to his Damon in a pastoral. Sir Aston Cokayne also addressed a complimentary poem to Rawson whom we may suppose he met on visits to his cousins' house when (as he puts it) Rawson abode in frozen Thule. Cotton seems to have kept in touch with his old tutor all his life : he mentions the Rollright Stones in a poem probably written in the severe winter of 1682–1683, and Rawson was Rector of Great Rollright from 1667 until his death in 1684. He too, like the Cottons and Cokaynes and Stanhopes, was a vigorous Royalist. Anthony Wood says that he animated his party by his preaching, and in 1659 he was implicated in Sir George Booth's plot, for which 'he narrowly escaped the halter'.

Many of Cotton's poems, as of Cokayne's, are outspoken in their detestation of Cromwell's dictatorship, and these were transcribed (probably by Richard Lovelace's younger brother Dudley) in a manuscript book which once belonged to his neighbours the Fitzherberts. Most of the poems in this collection were written in Cotton's youth, before the Restoration, and were intended to please his like-minded friends. His earliest poem, on the death of the young Lord Hastings, had already been published in 1649 in *Lachrymae*

Musarum, alongside Dryden's first published poem and others by Herrick and Marvell and Denham, Cokayne, Brome, and Bancroft. Two years later he contributed a poem in commendation of his friend Edmund Prestwich's translation of Seneca's *Hippolytus*. The earliest poem in the Fitzherbert manuscript is an elegy on Lord Derby, who was taken prisoner after the Battle of Worcester and beheaded on 15 October 1651. Cotton here, as always, is very outspoken :

> *To what a formidable greatness grown*
> *Is this prodigious beast, Rebellion,*

he begins, and the poem is less a lament for Derby than an execration upon his murderers. Poems such as this, or as the burlesque *Litany*, which must date from about the same time, would have brought him into serious trouble had they been circulated outside the group of loyal Derbyshire families, Stanhopes, Cokaynes, Ports, Fitzherberts, who were his friends. But they must have heartened and delighted them.

> *From a ruler that's a curse,*
> *And a government that's worse ;*
> *From a prince that rules by awe,*
> *Whose tyrannic will's his law ;*
> *From an armed council board,*
> *And a sceptre that's a sword.*
> Libera nos *etc.*

Cotton's scorn of the turncoat Waller is strident : no doubt he preferred the more robust company of poets such as Tom Weaver, Thomas Bancroft, and Alexander Brome. To the last he addressed epistles in verse, and Brome replied in kind, writing from London which he considered 'no place for verse', where poets must invoke the Muses which, at Beresford, rather themselves courted Cotton :

> *You and your house contribute to each other :*
> *Such hills, such dales, such plains, such rocks, such springs,*
> *And such a confluence of all such things*
> *As raise and gratify the Muses.*

Alexander Brome, who engaged his Muse in the cause of the Cavaliers with heartening song and satire, was a visitor to Beresford Hall and knew Izaak Walton, who contributed a pastoral poem 'written the 29 of May 1660' (to celebrate King Charles's return to London that day) to Brome's collected *Songs and other Poems* published the following year.

Another and finer poet, the loyal and gallant Richard Lovelace, had been a close friend of Cotton's family for years ; had addressed a poem, *The Grasshopper*, to Cotton's father, and had written an elegy on his aunt Cassandra. When Lovelace was in need therefore, Cotton sent him twenty shillings every Monday morning for some months on end, and at another time, perhaps during the rule of the Major-Generals in August 1655, concealed him from pursuit in the secret caves of Dovedale, as Lovelace acknowledged :

> *What fate was mine when in mine obscure cave*
> *(Shut up almost close prisoner in a grave)*
> *Your beams could reach me through this vault of night,*
> *And canton the dark dungeon with light.*

Later in the autumn of 1655 Cotton went to the Continent, for the only time in his life, having received a licence to travel with Francis Cholmondeley 'for improvement of their studies'. He visited France and Holland, and perhaps Italy. But he had additional reasons now for the homesickness which always seized him when he was away from Beresford. Before he left England he had fallen in love with his cousin Isabella Hutchinson, and indeed their families' objection to the marriage on the grounds of kinship may have been one reason for sending him abroad at this time. He complains of this in a poem called *The Separation* :

> *But oh ! the unwelcome cause*
> *Of superstitious laws !*
> *That us from our mutual embraces tear,*
> *And separate our bloods, because too near.*

And in another poem he laments their need to run in separate courses,

> *The fiction incest so to shun.*

He took her picture with him, a miniature no doubt to be gazed on in secret during his absence in France. (Later he was on friendly terms with the poet and miniaturist Thomas Flatman, but in 1655 Flatman was no more than eighteen, and, so far as we know, had not yet started painting.) On this subject too Cotton wrote a charming *Ode* which he sent to her from France.

> *In dark and melancholy groves,*
> *Where pretty birds discourse their loves,*
> > *I daily worship on my knee*
> > *Thy shadow — all I have of thee —*
> > *And sue to that to pity me.*
>
> *I vow to it the sacred vow*
> *To thee, and only thee, I owe ;*
> > *When (as it knew my true intent)*
> > *The silent picture gives consent,*
> > *And seems to mourn my banishment. . . .*
>
> *And though thy shadow here take place,*
> *By intimating future grace,*

It goes before, but to impart
To thee, how beautiful thou art,
And show a reason for my smart.

Nor is't improper, sweet, since thou
Art in thy youthful morning now,
Whilst I deprived of thine eyes' light,
Do drooping live a tedious night,
In Paris, like an anchorite.

Isabella, whose half-brother the Roundhead Colonel wooed his Lucy with similar romantic sentiment, surely was moved to tears on receiving this. Their story had a happy ending, for on Cotton's return their devotion to one another overcame their families' discouragement, and they were married in St Mary's Church, Nottingham, on 30 June 1656. To celebrate their wedding Lovelace wrote *The Triumphs of Philamore and Amoret*, in which he alludes to the help Cotton had given him not long before, and describes the civilized life which even in those sad times prevailed at Beresford Hall,

Where now each à la mode inhabitant,
Himself and 's manners both do pay you rent,
And 'bout your house (your palace) doth resort
And 'spite of fate and war creates a court.

This is the last poem by Lovelace that can be dated, for he was dead by October 1657. When in 1660 with the Restoration Dudley Lovelace could publish a volume of elegies in his brother's memory, among these Cotton's poem takes pride of place. It is a deservedly generous tribute, in the best Augustan manner

To pay my love to thee, and pay it so
As honest men should what they justly owe,
Were to write better of thy life than can

The assured'st pen of the most worthy man :
Such was thy composition, such thy mind
Improved to virtue, and from vice refined ;
Thy youth an abstract of the world's best parts,
Inured to arms and exercised in arts ;
Which with the vigour of a man became
Thine and thy country's pyramids of flame ;
Two glorious lights to guide our hopeful youth
Into the paths of honour and of truth,
These parts (so rarely met) made up in thee
What man should in his full perfection be.

In the meantime Charles and Isabella returned after their marriage to live at Beresford Hall. His mother had been dead four or five years, but his father was still living, one whose age (so Clarendon says) was 'less reverenced than his youth had been, and gave his best friends cause to have wished that he had not lived so long'. Whether or not he remained at Beresford after his son's marriage, there is nothing to suggest that Charles shared this severe judgment on his father, or that they were on any but the best of terms till the old man's death in 1658. Charles and Isabella lived quietly at home, where she bore him three sons and six daughters, of whom one son, Beresford Cotton, and four daughters survived the perils of infancy. Isabella died in 1669 and was buried in the village church of Alstonefield, where the pew in which she had used to sit for worship with her husband and children still remains.

The years of their marriage seem to have been content and little troubled. The hated Commonwealth crumbled and King Charles returned. The Royalists could again express freely opinions which up to now they had to confine to songs sung together in each other's houses, or to verses passed from hand to hand. Cotton celebrated the Restoration with a prose *Panegyrick*, — 'the worst panegyric that ever was writ', in the opinion of an anonymous poet of the time. But he could begin now to play his proper part in the local government of his High Peak : he became a revenue commissioner for the counties of Derbyshire and Staffordshire in 1660, and a magistrate in 1665. Two years later he was given a captain's commission in his cousin Lord Chesterfield's regiment. And once at least, in 1664, he visited London, when he had to apply to Parliament for financial relief.

Intermittent poverty, with the unwelcome persistence of creditors, were to be more or less constant troubles in his later years. His estate had already been impoverished by his father's extravagance before ever he succeeded to it, and Charles, who was too easy-going and generous to be a capable manager, was often hard up. The details of his debts and of his attempts to meet them are tedious and unimportant compared with the affectionate generosity of his relations which is now and then disclosed. He mentions his distresses a number of times in his poems, sadly or humorously, as the mood takes him, in a Pindarick ode in Cowley's manner on *Poverty*, in poems to friends or in the Horatian poem *Contentation* addressed to Izaak Walton, where he reflects on the little that will satisfy an honest and a grateful heart.

> *That man is happy in his share,*
>   *Who is warm clad, and cleanly fed,*
> *Whose necessaries bound his care,*
>   *And honest labour makes his bed.*
>
> *Who free from debt, and clear from crimes,*
>   *Honours those laws that others fear,*
> *Who ill of princes in worst times*
>   *Will neither speak himself nor hear.*

Who from the busy world retires,
To be more useful to it still,
And to no greater good aspires,
But only the eschewing ill.

It is an ideal which would hardly have met with the approval of his great contemporary Milton, yet there is something here to appeal to Wordsworth.

He wrote a begging letter in verse to Lord Chesterfield, who promised him a company of foot, with £300 a year, in the service of the Duke of Ormonde, Lord Lieutenant of Ireland, who was Chesterfield's father-in-law. Unluckily for Cotton, Ormonde was just at this very time deprived of his office, so that, though he set out for Ireland, nothing came of this commission except for a Burlesque which contains one of Cotton's engaging self-portraits. This vain journey to Ireland took place in May 1670, and we may suppose that, in spite of his recent widowhood and his need of the promised £300 a year, he returned home with a lighter heart than he set out.

Four years later Cotton married again, and though his wife, the Dowager Countess of Ardglass (who was related to Cromwell) had a considerable estate of her own, this does not seem to have freed him from debt. A few months after their marriage he had to apply to Parliament again for relief, to meet debts of £8000 through the sale of land held by his trustees. Worst of all his misfortunes came in 1681 when he was forced to sell his beloved Beresford Hall. But it was immediately bought back by his cousin John Beresford of Newton Grange, who allowed Charles to go on living there till his death in 1687. His son, Beresford Cotton, also seems to have lived there after him, for the indefatigable Celia Fiennes, riding that way in 1697, mentions 'a very exact house and gardens ; it's brick and coigned with stone, the gardens and courts very complete' which belonged to a Mr Cotton, J.P.

The house itself was pulled down in 1856, though the Beacon Tower has since been rebuilt. This Charles Cotton had put up to guide him home across the dark moors from Ashbourne, 'my Hero's Tower' he calls it in an epistle to his friend John Bradshaw in which he describes his journey home from London, by St Albans, Dunstable, Brickhill, Towcester, Lichfield, and Uttoxeter.

> *And there the Wednesday, being market-day,*
> *I was constrained with some kind lads to stay*
> *Tippling till afternoon, which made it night*
> *When from my Hero's Tower I saw the light*
> *Of her flambeaux, and fancied as we drave*
> *Each rising hillock was a swelling wave,*
> *And that I swimming was in Neptune's spite*
> *To my long longed-for harbour of delight.*

The house itself was a gabled L-shaped house, built early in the seventeenth century on rising ground on the right, or Staffordshire, bank of the river. It was surrounded by woods of Cotton's own planting. 'The pleasantness of the river, mountains and meadows about it cannot be described,' said Walton, 'unless Sir Philip Sidney, or Mr. Cotton's father, were alive again to do it,'

When Sir Henry Ellis, Librarian of the British Museum, visited Beresford Hall in 1814 he found it already sadly dilapidated, but little altered since the poet's time. The Parlour, he says, was 'wainscoted in small squares or panels ; in the window were two coats of arms, in ovals, of stained glass', the arms of Cotton and Beresford. Cokayne, in dedicating to Cotton *A Chain of Golden Poems* asked him to give his book 'leave to lie in your Parlour-window' where, he must have known, many of his cousin's guests would turn over its pleasant pages.

Several drawings of Beresford Hall, by John Linnell, Thomas Stothard, Clarkson Stanfield, and others, have been used to illustrate various editions of *The Compleat Angler*. Cotton himself was painted by Lely in 1657, shortly after his first marriage ; again perhaps by Lely some ten or twelve years later, this time in armour, to record his commission in Lord Chesterfield's regiment ; and thirdly by Edmund Ashfield in 1674, when Cotton had reached a middle-aged heaviness which four years before he had improbably attributed to sorrow —

For sorrow had made me a cumbersome burden.

We can thus very easily picture the handsome and friendly squire, after his breakfast of beer and a pipe of tobacco, talking to his steward, his miller, his tenants, and his neighbours in 'Basford Hall' as they all pronounced it,

Gravely inquiring how ewes are a score,
How the hay harvest and the corn was got.
And if or no there's like to be a rot.

We may be sure that his men served him well, for he had the courtesy to keep a regular routine : as he said, they 'knew his certain hours'. He might depreciate himself to the friend whom he had just left in London, as a 'dull Northern clod', but he was perfectly content with his 'cottage', and with his life there, and not at all envious of his more successful and fashionable friends. But he had the humour to see himself often enough as they saw him, that God-sent, unromantic gift with which men of his century and of the previous century were more often blessed than are we.

To be content with the life to which he was born was as great good fortune as to have been born to such a life, and Cotton was too intelligent, too active in mind and body, ever to grow complacent. 'Hearty, cheerful Mr. Cotton', Charles Lamb called him, and the epithets, however insufficient, are apt. He had cause enough for melancholy, the Civil War, ending in the defeat of his and his friends' hopes ; the discord between his mother and father ; the continual pestering of debts inherited from his father ; the early death of his first wife, and of several of their children ; the enforced sale of Beresford Hall. But Charles Cotton could always find refreshment of the spirit by his beloved river Dove, and, because he is a poet, he shares his pleasures with us still as generously as, in his lifetime, he shared them with all who came to visit him. That is just what he does : he invites us home with him as he invited Viator, the traveller met by the way, and with a friendly smile he watches us as we cross the pack-horse bridge ('Why, a mouse can hardly go over it : 'tis not two fingers broad') or sweat up Hanson Toot. He is always delighted to introduce his country to yet another visitor, and to share their surprise at its unexpected quality. For it is surprising country, with its bleak open moorland suddenly cleft into deep, ash-grown dales ; with its caves and its pot-holes, its 'tidal' spring and shifting mountain, and all the other wonders of the Peak ; with rivers like Lathkill and Manifold that flow sometimes in and sometimes under their stony channels. ('Nonsense !' said Dr Johnson, and could not be persuaded to go far enough out of Ashbourne to see for himself.) He even rejoices, with a lively irony far removed from Charles Kingsley's tiresome heartiness, in winter and rough weather. Wordsworth especially admired the *Winter Quatrains* for 'a profusion of fanciful comparisons, which indicate on the part of the poet extreme activity of intellect, and a corresponding hurry of delightful feeling'. And, after safeguarding his reputation by a declaration that he himself was a teetotaller, Wordsworth transcribes forty lines from the poem in praise of the insulating (and other) powers of wine.

> 'Tis that, that gives the poet rage,
> And thaws the gelid blood of age,
> Matures the young, restores the old,
> And makes the fainting coward bold.

> It lays the careful head to rest,
> Calms palpitations in the breast,
> Renders our lives' misfortunes sweet,
> And Venus frolic in the sheet.*

> We'll think of all the friends we know,
> And drink to all worth drinking to :
> When, having drunk all thine and mine,
> We rather shall want healths than wine.

He can write a rollicking drinking song, too, to sing with his friends in derision of canting Puritans.

> Let me have sack, tobacco store,
> A drunken friend, a little whore, —
> Protector ! I will ask no more !

And he will tell in verse some anecdote of local fame such as he must often have told to his friends, imitating (as we may be sure that he could) the dialect of High Peak folk. So in *The Wonders of the Peak* he recounts the story of a country fellow who one night rode his mare over the cliff at Peak Castle, yet lived to tell the tale when he got back home.

* The one-time lover of Annette Vallon, with a further tenderness for reputation, omitted this line from his transcription.

Thither he comes, and knocking at the door
(Though not so hard as he was knocked before)
His master hears at first, and cries 'Who's there ?'
'Why' (poorly cries the other) 'I am here.'
Up starts the master straight, and lets him in :
'I'th' name of God,' (quoth he,) 'where hast thou bin
That thou'rt thus late ?'   To which the wise reply
Was this, 'Nay, master, what the dee'l know I ?
But somewhere I have had a lungeous faw,
I'm sure o' that.   And, master, that's neet aw.'
A candle then was lighted, when his sconce
Did represent Raw-head and Bloody-bones.
'A lungeous fall, indeed,' the master said,
'Thy very looks would make a man afraid,
Thou hast drunk deep thy hogs-head on the tilt.
— But where's my mare ?'   'No matter where.   Hoo's kilt,'
Replies the man, 'i'th' morninck send and see,
The devil's power go with these tors for me.'

But in the morning the mare too was found safe and sound.

Sans hurt or blemish, save a little strip
Of hair and skin rippled upon her hip.

From this Cotton moves on easily to describe the seventh of
the Wonders of the Peak, Chatsworth, 'this palace, with
wild prospects girded round' he calls it in his first line, at
once noting that astonishing contrast between splendid
civilized house and wild surroundings which can hardly be
discovered outside the British isles.   He remembers Bess of
Hardwick's old house which had recently been pulled down,
and he contrasts the two in apt metaphor of feminine fashions
of dress.

Thy foundress dressed thee in such robes as they
In those old fashioned times reputed gay,
Of which new stripped, and the old rustling pride
Of ruff and farthingale now laid aside,
Thy shapes appear, and thou thyself art seen
A very Christian, and a modish Queen.

And he is forced to admit, 'though old friends part ill', that he prefers the new Chatsworth :

I needs must say, for I have seen both faces,
Thou'rt much more lovely in the modern graces.

The whole of this final passage of *The Wonders of the Peak* can stand comparison with other seventeenth-century poems about country houses, Ben Jonson's of Penshurst, Thomas Carew's of Saxham, even Andrew Marvell's of Appleton House. For Charles Cotton of Beresford Hall, unlike the others, wrote as an owner of a country house (however small and homely) not as a visitor to one, wrote therefore with the intimacy of one who appreciated such practical details as the lighting of a room or the easy gradient of a staircase. Most of all, perhaps, he appreciates the lay-out of the gardens, with their fountains, cascades, statues, and terraces, for were not his own gardens at Beresford 'very complete' ? In these things he was a connoisseur.

Thus did he make poetry out of the life of an English country gentleman, the life of houses and gardens, of sport and politics and military service, of farming and the planting of woods and orchards ; above all, a life full of friends with whom to talk about all these things, in his own house or in theirs. The poem which Cotton addressed to Izaak Walton on 17 January 1672, and which Walton printed with the next edition of his *Lives*, is an epistle on friendship, which he took to be the origin of the biographies of Donne, Wotton, and Herbert; and it ends with the hope that he himself might be remembered as a friend of Walton.

> *But, my dear friend, 'tis so, that you and I,*
> *By a condition of mortality,*
> *With all this great, and more proud world, must die.*
>
> *In which estate, I ask no more of fame,*
> *Nor other monument of honour claim,*
> *Than that of your true friend to advance my name.*

How pleased Cotton would be to know with what certainty his hope has been fulfilled.

TEXTS

Poems, ed. John Beresford, Cobden-Sanderson, 1923.
Poems, ed. John Buxton (Muses' Library), Routledge & Kegan Paul, 1958 (makes use of a contemporary MS. unknown to Beresford).

8

THE COUNTESS OF
WINCHILSEA

A NNE FINCH, Countess of Winchilsea, the first English
woman to write poetry that no man could have written,
found her best inspiration in the domestic happiness of her
marriage, in the retired life which she shared with her husband on the family's estate in Kent, and in the social round
of visits to their friends. She was born in April 1661, the
youngest of the three children of Sir William Kingsmill, a
Hampshire baronet of long descent. Her father died when
she was but five months old, and her mother (who had re-
married) when she was no more than three, so that for her
upbringing and education she must have been in the care of
some relation. Most probably her mother's brother Sir
William Haselwood, of Maidwell in Northamptonshire,
looked after her. By 1683 she was at Court, a Maid of
Honour to the Duchess of York, Mary of Modena, along
with the lively and clever Susanna Lady Belasyse and Catherine Sedley, and Anne Killigrew whose death from small-
pox at the age of twenty-five Dryden was to lament in a
famous Pindarick ode. Anne Killigrew was a pupil of Lely,
and her self-portrait before her posthumous *Poems* shows that
she had a remarkable gift ; she was also, so Dryden says,
skilled in painting landscape. As a poet she showed no sign
of femininity, but wrote like a man, just as Katherine Philips

'the matchless Orinda' had lately written, or as Aphra Behn
was writing. The two young Maids of Honour must
have known each other intimately, and (we may suppose) discussed poetry together, but there is nothing in
common between the poems they wrote, and so far as we
know Anne Kingsmill wrote little poetry until after her
marriage.

   Captain the Honourable Heneage Finch, later Lieutenant-
Colonel in the Coldstream Guards, Gentleman of the Bed-
Chamber to the Duke of York, met Anne Kingsmill at Court.
He had not then any expectation of succeeding to the Earl-
dom, and must have looked forward to a life devoted to the
service of the heir to the throne, just as Anne must have
expected to spend her life at Court. They were married at
St Martin-in-the-Fields on 15 May 1684 : Captain Finch
was twenty-seven, and Anne, by a demure subtraction of
five years, described herself on the marriage licence as 'about
eighteen'. The marriage, though childless, was entirely
happy, and thirty-nine years later, when Anne had been dead
nearly three years, the elderly Lord Winchilsea noted in his
diary : 'May 15, 1684. Most blessed day.' For the first
few years of their married life they lived in Westminster,
most unfashionably content with one another. The accession
of James in February 1685 must have increased Colonel
Finch's duties at Court ; he also became a Deputy Lieutenant
for the county of Kent, and sat for two years in Parliament as
member for Hythe. But the Revolution of 1688 brought
all this life of Court and city to an end for them both, since
Colonel Finch was a man of too high principles and of too
devoted a loyalty to the House of Stuart to be able to take
the oath of allegiance to Dutch William. We may be
sure that the equally high-minded Anne approved his decision.

In the spring of 1690 Colonel Finch was arrested while on his way to France, but soon released again. For a time he and his wife seem to have stayed with various members of their families in different country houses, at Kirby, Godmersham, Hothfield, Wye, and Eastwell, but after two or three years the young Earl of Winchilsea, who had succeeded his grandfather in 1689, invited them to make their permanent home with him at Eastwell. In 1712 he died and Heneage Finch succeeded his nephew as fifth Earl. Eastwell was at that time a sixteenth-century house, begun in Henry VIII's time by Sir Thomas Moyle, whose daughter Catherine's marriage to Thomas Finch brought it into the possession of that family. In 1589 their son, Sir Moyle Finch, who married the heiress of Sir Thomas Heneage, enlarged and embattled Eastwell. It was set in a park on the North Downs whose slopes were well furnished with ancient oaks, beeches, and yews, and from a rise known as Mount Pleasant there was a view over the rich Kent countryside even as far, on a clear day, as the English Channel. Later in the century the old house was swept away, and, of the buildings Lady Winchilsea knew, only the grand flint and ashlar gatehouse by the road from Ashford to Faversham remains. Thus the house which was to be her home for thirty years, and where she wrote most of her poetry, was an Elizabethan mansion, one which (in spite of certain improvements effected in the early 1700s) her more elegant friends would have considered as old-fashioned and *démodé* as her devotion to James II and Mary of Modena, her preference for life in the country to life in London, her untroubled happiness in her marriage. But from these sources she derived poetry which could win the admiration of both Pope and Wordsworth.

From the first Captain Finch, undismayed by the prospect of being known as the husband of a Female Wit, encouraged her to write poetry. If he had to be away for the day, he delighted to find a copy of verses on his return, and on the rare occasions when they were separated for longer she was to write her letters to him in verse. In the summer of 1685, a year after their marriage, she went to Tunbridge Wells to take the waters, but Captain Finch, miserable at her absence, begged her to return. She replied in verse:

> *Daphnis, your wish no more repeat*
> *For my return, nor mourn my stay,*
> *Lest my wise purpose you defeat,*
> *And urged by love I come away.*
> *My own desires I can resist,*
> *But blindly yield if you persist.*

The affectionate playfulness is very characteristic, and so too, in spite of the pastoral affectation of addressing her husband as Daphnis, is the direct, plain style. (Daphnis was matched in her poems with Ardelia, by which perhaps she meant to suggest the ardour of her own disposition.) But she had a humorous perception of the absurdity of being a blue-stocking in Restoration England, and of the still greater absurdity of addressing love-poems to her own husband. So in 1689, writing a poem to please him on his return home one evening, she summoned the Muses to her aid, and told them that for the matter of her poem, she wished to rehearse a husband's praise.

> *A Husband! ecchoed all around:*
> *And to Parnassus sure that sound*
> *   Had never yet been sent;*
> *Amazement in each face was read,*
> *In haste the affrighted sisters fled,*
> *   And unto council went.*

Erato cried, since Grizel's days,
Since Troy-town pleased, and Chevy-chase,
No such design was known ;
And 'twas their business to take care
It reached not to the public ear
Or got about the town.

The town indeed (as she suggests in the same poem) had been exhausting its wit with hastily written panegyrics to the usurper William. But at this time she had no thought of publishing her poems, and the fashionable world from which Ardelia and Daphnis had been abruptly exiled must be denied the privilege of laughing at them :

We own (who in the Muse delight)
'Tis for ourselves, not them, we write.

No doubt the serious-minded Daphnis nodded his assent.

Deprived, by his own decision, of the public career to which his birth naturally entitled him, Colonel Finch devoted himself to those intellectual interests which to him, as to his wife, were more congenial. He could not interfere with the running of Eastwell, and it says much for his tact that there is never any hint of friction between himself and the young Earl during the twenty years and more that he lived as a guest in the house where he had spent his childhood. He studied mathematics as well as literature and history, and he amused himself by painting. Sometimes, perhaps, as a man bred to court and camp might do, he would regret the idle life he led, and remember the aristocratic tradition that (as Sidney had said) 'the end of all earthly learning is virtuous action'. But then Anne would come and entice him out of doors 'to take the pleasures of the fields with her'.

When such a day blessed the Arcadian plain,
Warm without sun, and shady without rain,
Fanned by an air that scarcely bent the flowers
Or waved the woodbines on the summer bowers,
The nymphs disordered beauty could not fear,
Nor ruffling winds uncurled the shepherds' hair,
On the fresh grass they trod their measures light
And a long evening made, from noon to night.
Come then, my Daphnis, from those cares descend
Which better may the winter season spend.
  Come, and the pleasures of the fields survey,
    And through the groves with your Ardelia stray . . .
As Baucis and Philemon spent their lives,
Of husbands he, the happiest she of wives,
When through the painted meads their way they sought,
Harmless in act and unperplexed in thought,
Let us, my Daphnis, rural joys pursue,
And Courts or Camps not even in fancy view.
  So let us through the groves, my Daphnis, stray,
    And so the pleasures of the fields survey.

Daphnis, we may be certain, willingly obeyed.

Ardelia herself, with no masculine tradition of the active
life to make discontent, with no household to manage, and no
children to care for, might yet have found time hang heavy
on her, had she not taken endless pleasure in the life of the
countryside. Once, on a visit to Eastwell in July 1689, she
took too long a walk in the park, drawn (she said) by 'romantic notions', and got a lift home again 'in a water-cart driven
by one of the underkeepers in his green coat, with a hazel-
bough for a whip'. She turned the incident into a burlesque,
merrily laughing at herself for so unromantic a homecoming.
She loved the park, which she thought the finest in England,

so much that she felt her gift of poetry unequal to the task of
its description : if only it had been otherwise, she would
surely have exalted its fame above Denham's *Cooper's Hill*.
In any event, as she told Pope, she always found it difficult
to praise well what she admired. But when in 1702 Lord
Winchilsea (her nephew) undertook various improvements
at Eastwell she celebrated the occasion in verse. Among
these works was the conversion of a mount, that typically
Elizabethan feature of a large garden, into a terrace :

> *So lies this hill, hewn from its rugged height,*
> *Now levelled to a scene of smooth delight,*
> *Where on a terrace of its spoils we walk*
> *And of the task and the performer talk.*

She preferred the distant, unimpeded view which the new
terrace gave to surveying elaborately formal knots from the
elevation of the mount, just as she preferred the enlarged
windows which were inserted in the old house at the same
time. In these things she shared the taste of the coming age
rather than of that which had passed.

Fifty years before, Andrew Marvell had written his longest
poem in compliment to Lord Fairfax, about the house and
gardens and park at Nunappleton in Yorkshire. But he preferred the military precision of formal gardening and would
not have liked the new landscaping which Lord Winchilsea
was bringing to Eastwell ; and he never gave any hint that
he had looked beyond the confines of the park to 'beauteous
fields and scattered woods', or to the remote moorlands in
the distance. Yet it is Marvell's poetry that Lady Winchilsea's most often recalls, not because Marvell's tense power of
phrase and precise brilliance of imagery lack virility — far
from it — but because in an age of fanaticism Marvell remained a balanced and civilized being, one who appreciated

the art of living so well that he could declare a cause 'too good to have been fought for'. His achievement was the greater partly because it was so much more difficult in the 1650s than in the 1700s, for a man than for a woman, to refuse to be diverted by the trivialities of political passion.

Marvell's *Garden*, or the park of Appleton House, where he found seclusion from the turmoils of the time, are not unlike the ideal world which Lady Winchilsea describes in her *Petition for an Absolute Retreat*. They wrote in similar situations ; Marvell when he had joined Lord Fairfax in retirement after his refusal to lead Cromwell's armies against the Scots, Lady Winchilsea when she had accompanied her husband after his refusal to come to terms with 'the Glorious Revolution'. If Marvell had found himself where

> *Grapes with juice so crowded up*
> *As breaking through the native cup,*
> *Figs, yet growing, candied o'er*
> *By the sun's attracting power,*
> *Cherries, with the downy peach,*
> *All within my easy reach,*

he would not have thought himself a stranger, though he and his hostess would not have agreed about the company they wished to keep. To Marvell

> *Two paradises 'twere in one*
> *To live in paradise alone.*

But Lady Winchilsea included in her *Petition* this :

> *Give me there (since heaven has shown*
> *It was not good to be alone)*
> *A partner suited to my mind,*
> *Solitary, pleased, and kind ;*

Who, partially, may something see
Preferred to all the world in me.

Marvell, nostalgic for the primal innocence of Eden, must dissent from the longings of Eve and her daughters.

The Petition for an Absolute Retreat is one of the longest and most ambitious of Lady Winchilsea's poems ; it is also one of the best. Like many of her poems it is addressed to a friend (here, to the Countess of Thanet,*) whose company she would welcome in her retreat from the world of fashion. It was that world with its talk of business, and wars, its news and rumours, its exotic dishes and extravagant dress, its attitudes and affectations — in a word, its vanity, that she rejected. Not there could she feel at home, but on some quiet estate in the country. She was thoroughly English in her tastes and preferred the peace of the garden to the frivolity of London, preferred also (we may be sure) country clothes to London finery, so that to her smart acquaintance she was

> *so rustic in her clothes and mien,*
> *'Tis with her ungenteel to be seen.*

We might imagine her, in our own day, dressed in a tweed suit, a Henry Heath hat and flat-heeled shoes, busy about her herbaceous borders, a flower-basket on her arm and seca-teurs in her hand, arranging the flowers in the house, and managing her household with calm competence, yet finding time to be well read and to enjoy the conversation of her friends and guests.

She wrote *The Petition* at a time of distress when all she wished was to creep away from the hostile world which had

---

* She was Catherine Cavendish, and married at the age of nineteen in 1684. The Earl of Thanet's seat, Hothfield Place, was only a couple of miles or so from Eastwell Park.

caused this. Later, when she had recovered her spirits, she could gaily deride that world with a sharpness of perception which suggests Jane Austen. *Ardelia's Answer to Ephelia*, who had invited her to come to her in town, like *The Petition*, could only have been written by a woman. She disclaims any bent for the satire and detraction that were all the rage : she had not, she says (and we may believe her), enough ill-nature joined to her wit. She portrays Almeria as another Melantha, to whose distaste, when they go on an expedition, she presently stops the coach for, of all things, to go into a church. The scene is drawn with delightful felicity. We are shown Almeria fluttering at the windows of her coach in her eagerness to attract attention. Thus

> *the gay thing, light as her feathered dress,*
> *Flies round the coach, and does each cushion press ;*
> *Through every glass her several graces shows,*
> *This, does her face, and that, her shape expose*
> *To envying beauties and admiring beauxs.*
> *One stops and, as expected, all extols,*
> *Clings to the door and on his elbow lolls,*
> *Thrusts in his head, at once to view the fair*
> *And keep his curls from discomposing air,*
> *Then thus proceeds —*
>   *'My wonder it is grown*
> *To find Almeria here, and here alone.*
> *Where are the nymphs that round you used to crowd,*
> *Of your long courted approbation proud,*
> *Learning from you, how to erect their hair,*
> *And in perfection all their habit wear,*
> *To place a patch in some peculiar way,*
> *That may an unmarked smile to sight betray,*
> *And the vast genius of the Sex display ?'*

'Pity me then (she cries) and learn the fate
That makes me porter to a temple gate.'

And Almeria gives her beau a portrait of the wretched
Ardelia : she is most tiresomely uninterested in Almeria's
efforts to make something of her ; disdains her advice on
how to dress, or where to shop ; fails to remark on the
excellence of the tea she is given to drink ; refuses to prefer
the latest plays to those of dull old authors like Dryden,
Etherege, and Lee. Besides, Ardelia has such out of date
ideas on feminine beauty or masculine wit, is so Puritanical,
so boorish. This contrast of sense and sensibility has lost
nothing of its freshness or point ; and the author of *Mis-*
cellany Poems on several occasions, written by a Lady, 1713,
deserves to be remembered with the author of a novel 'by a
Lady' which was published in three volumes in 1811.

As with Jane Austen, Lady Winchilsea's comments on vain
women have a feminine sharpness of rebuke quite unlike
what we find in Congreve or Pope. She felt that such as
Almeria were a disgrace to her sex, and thought it undignified
that men should find them amusing. In a poem which she
wrote when on a visit to Tunbridge Wells in 1706, where
she discovered an affectation of surprise at a young man
being in love, she gave some advice to the young ladies :

For every fop lay not the insnaring train,
Nor lose the worthy to allure the vain,
Keep at due distance all attempts of bliss,
Nor let too near a whisper seem a kiss.
Be not the constant partner of a swain,
Except his long address that favour gain ;
Nor be transported when some trifle's view
Directs his giddy choice to fix on you.

The Ephelia who had invited Ardelia to visit London was probably a member of the Thynne family of Longleat, but if such invitations were unacceptable, invitations to their magnificent house in Wiltshire were welcome. In an epistle to Lady Worsley 'who had most obligingly desired my corresponding with her by letters', Ardelia briefly mentions the famous house

Which above metaphor its structure rears,

but chiefly commends the gardens with their fountains, terraces, and lawns, in order to compliment Lord and Lady Weymouth * (the parents of the newly married Lady Worsley) on the taste they had there shown in laying out the gardens in the new Dutch style. Lady Winchilsea felt more at ease in commenting on the gardens, as she did even at Eastwell, than on the house and its contents, especially in view of the reputation as a connoisseur deservedly enjoyed by Viscount Weymouth's son Henry, the Theanor of Ardelia's poems. His excellent taste (she tells us)

> *Italy has wrought*
> *In his refined and daily heightened thought,*
> *Where poetry or painting find no place*
> *Unless performed with a superior grace.*

And perhaps she took the greater pleasure in strolling through the newly improved grounds with her host and hostess, when

> *'Twas paradise in some expanded walk*
> *To see her motions and attend his talk.*

However, though she eschewed the harder labour of describing Longleat, she did attempt a description of one of

* She was daughter of the third Earl of Winchilsea and thus Lady Worsley was Colonel Finch's niece.

the tapestries in the house in a poem addressed to Henry
Thynne ; and in another she rebuked the painter of an ill-
drawn picture of his wife. She knew the Henry Thynnes at
Longleat, and she also visited them at their house at Leweston
in Dorset from which she dated a letter in 1704 to Lady
Worsley, enclosing a fragment of a Pindarick ode in which
she compared Longleat to Armida's Castle. This was particu-
larly apt, because it was almost certainly Henry Thynne who
translated literally to her those passages from Tasso which
she turned into verse.

Lady Winchilsea showed her poems to Henry Thynne for
criticism, as she says in some lines addressed to his daughter
(who married Lord Hertford in 1715) where she requests her to

> *look with favour on Ardelia's muse,*
> *And what your father cherished, still excuse.*
> *Whenever style or fancy in them shines,*
> *Conclude his praise gave spirit to those lines.*

Lady Hertford inherited her father's critical judgment, for in
1728 James Thomson dedicated to her his *Spring* which (he
said) 'grew up under her encouragement' ; and she also be-
friended Savage and Shenstone. But Lady Winchilsea in a
poem addressed to her when she had engaged Eusden 'to
write upon a wood, enjoining him to mention no tree but the
aspen and no flower but the king-cup' light-heartedly asserted
a romantic liberty for the poet against the patron,

> *For we're all wronged if Eusden is confined.*

This poem well illustrates the incipient romanticism which
Wordsworth so much valued in Lady Winchilsea's poetry.
In it she mischievously invents the kind of poem which the
poet laureate would have written but for Lady Hertford's
prescribed limitations.

Had Eusden been at liberty to rove,
Wild and promiscuous he had formed your grove
Of all the sons of earth that ever grew,
From lightsome beech down to the sable yew,

and she goes on to name lime, hazel, sycamore, maple, cedar, pine, juniper, hawthorn, holly, oak, birch, and ash. She even pretends to despise Lady Hertford's chosen tree which

Is but the rattle to some peevish wind.

Her own love of trees is often apparent, and though Wordsworth could not have read this poem (since even now it remains unpublished) one of his favourites was that entitled *The Tree*, in which she gives thanks for its shade and shelter, and prays that its end may come at last through the wind and not the axe. She had a particular reason, other than that of romantic sentiment, for disliking the felling of trees. Some years before she first came to Eastwell the then Earl of Winchilsea felled a grove of oaks, 'and gave the first blow with his own hands', John Aubrey records. 'Shortly after, the Countess died in her bed suddenly, and his eldest son, the Lord Maidstone, was killed at sea by a cannon-bullet.' This was in the Battle of Sole-Bay on 28 May 1672. He was serving on board the *Royal Charles* and his son Charles was born four months later. The association of the felling of the oaks with the deaths of her husband's mother and brother must have been very well known to her, and she alludes to it in the poem which she wrote on the improvements made by the fourth Earl, that same Lord Maidstone's son, from which I have already quoted. This story too, though it is not very likely that Wordsworth knew it, would have pleased the romantic taste for the supernatural.

Besides writing poems to her friends about their country houses and gardens, Lady Winchilsea would use her gift to

amuse their children, or to commemorate birthdays, marriages, and deaths. Among her more charming poems are
those to her friend Lady Thanet's children, Lady Catherine
and Lady Anne Tufton. Lady Catherine addressed to her
the first letter she ever wrote, and Lady Winchilsea replied
in verse congratulating her on 'sense and characters beyond
her years', and promising always to treasure it. To Lady
Anne she addressed a petition on behalf of a white mouse,
which may well have accompanied the gift of the first pet the
little girl had kept.

> *With all respect and humble duty*
> *And passing every mouse in beauty,*
> *With fur more white than garden lilies,*
> *And eyes as bright as any Phillis,*
> *I sue to wear Lamira's fetters*
> *And live the envy of my betters.*

Among the friends whose deaths she mourned were James
Thynne, the younger brother of Henry Thynne and of Lady
Worsley, and Sir William Twysden of Roydon Hall in
Kent, who was also related to her husband. This last is a
Pindarick of somewhat excessive length, but yet it reveals her
genuine admiration for a dear friend who was also a man of
fine manners and sound learning, worthy (at least in her eyes)
to be mourned as a second Astrophel. The best of her
elegiac writing is the short poem *To Death*. Here, for all the
range of emotion in the many noble apostrophes to Death
that had preceded it, is something new, for no man had contrived the same blend of faith and terror and pathos, of
timidity and pity and calm resolution as she does; and
perhaps no man had done so because no man had shared a
woman's view of death until Lady Winchilsea wrote her
sixteen simple lines.

So far I have been considering those poems which she made to please her husband and her friends. It was in these that she developed a talent which in the face of an unknown audience she would have been too shy even to discover. For her, as for so many in her day and before, the writing of poetry was one of the accomplishments that made life more delightful, also (perhaps) more intelligible, and, like Dryden, she thought that poetry should both teach and divert ; but she wrote principally because she enjoyed making verses. That is not to say that her poems lack substance : they reveal a woman who was glad to accept much in the life of her time, but who was far from submitting to standards which it might easily have imposed on a less strong character. She was not so much awed by the military glories of Marlborough's campaigns that she would share in worship at the 'mistaken shrine' of that 'false idol, honour'. To her war meant not the winning of fame, but the destruction and degradation of life, and she viewed this masculine world with disgust and pity. Neither would she concede that

> *a woman that attempts the pen*
> *Is an intruder on the rights of men.*

She saw no reason why a woman's utmost art and use should be 'the dull manage of a servile house', or why she should be restricted to accomplishments more customary than the writing of poetry. But in spite of her dislike for the way of life traditional for women of her class, she had no wish to invade man's province, and the best of her poems are the most feminine.

> *Whilst in the Muses' paths I stray,*
> *Whilst in their groves and by their secret springs,*
> *My hand delights to trace unusual things,*
> *And deviates from the known and common way ;*

172

> *Nor will in fading silks compose*
> *Faintly the inimitable rose,*
> *Fill up an ill-drawn bird, or paint on glass*
> *The sovereign's blurred and undistinguished face,*
> *The threatening angel, and the speaking ass.*

These lines come from her Pindarick Ode *The Spleen* which was published in Gildon's *Collection of Poems*, 1701. (This is not, as has often been said, her first appearance in print. Six religious poems by her, including two paraphrases, had been published in *Miscellanea Sacra*, 1696; but contribution to such an anthology might be regarded as a pious duty rather than as an attempt to establish a literary reputation.) Composition in so 'public' a form as Cowley's Pindarick must imply some intention to publish, however discreetly and anonymously, and a poet who could win the approval of such critics as Henry Thynne and Lord Mulgrave, Nicholas Rowe and Jonathan Swift, might well be ambitious to reach a wider circle than that of her family and friends. Rowe indeed had seen *The Spleen* and another Pindarick on the theme *All is Vanity* before 1701, when he wrote a verse *Epistle to Flavia on the sight of two Pindarick Odes . . . written by a Lady, her Friend.* (Later, Lady Winchilsea returned the compliment in *A Poem, occasioned by the sight of the 4th Epistle Lib. Epist. 1 of Horace . . . by Mr. Rowe, who had before sent hither, another translation from Horace.*) *All is Vanity* is probably earlier than *The Spleen*, but a third Pindarick Ode *On the Hurricane* was written immediately after the storm which it describes, which took place on 27 November 1703. In these odes Lady Winchilsea follows Cowley's prescription, for it was not until 1706 that Congreve attacked the form (which he too had used) as 'a bundle of rambling, incoherent thoughts, expressed in a like parcel of irregular stanzas', and proposed a return to the more correct form which Ben Jonson had attempted and which Gray was to follow in *The Bard* and *The Progress of Poesy*.

Of her three Odes *The Spleen* is the most successful. From it both Pope and Shelley borrowed a felicitous phrase. For the greatest poet of her own day it was the sophisticated rose of high summer that must bring aromatic pain, but for Lady Winchilsea, and for Shelley, the flower was the cool, fresh jonquil of spring. The contrast is not without its relevance for in writing on the Spleen Lady Winchilsea was writing of the characteristic female malady of the eighteenth century — that perennial affliction which Victorians called the Vapours, and which we call maladjustment (and send for the psychiatrist).

> Though the physician's greatest gains,
> Although his growing wealth he sees
> Daily increased by ladies' fees,
> Yet dost thou baffle all his studious pains.

But a contemporary physician thought well enough of Lady Winchilsea's description of the symptoms to reprint it in his treatise on the disease. Her age was uncertain whether reason should have absolute commandment, as the Elizabethans had said, or whether it is and ought only to be the slave of the passions, as Hume was soon to assert; but for Lady Winchilsea, as for Milton, the loss of innocence which led to this dispute was to be traced to the Fall of Man. The Spleen, she saw, was as much the cause of Almeria's follies,

> The careless posture, and the head reclined,

as of her own darker moods, when she would be ready to listen to the hostile criticism of her verses which, in other moods, she would merrily rebut.

Amateur poet she might be, and certainly so always thought of herself, but she was well read in the critics of the time, Dryden, Roscommon and Mulgrave, Rapin, Boileau, Dacier, and reflected upon her art with the intention always to write as well as she could. She translated from Tasso and Petrarch, from Racine and from La Fontaine, whose fables suggested to her a manner of writing when 'weary of the Pindarick way'. She was the first English follower of La Fontaine, preceding Gay, whose *Fables* were not published until some years after her death, by twenty years or more. It is surprising that she had no rivals for, as Addison said, La Fontaine was more in vogue than any other author of the time. She was well equipped for the writing of fables by her meticulous observation of birds and beasts and flowers and by her humour, so that *The Owl describing her Young Ones* does so with the lively delight that Lady Winchilsea must have felt when she saw

> *the pretty souls*
> *With waddling steps and frowzy polls*
> *Come creeping from their secret holes.*

Lady Winchilsea's observation of the human scene was no less acute, and the poem has its moral for fond mothers who overpraise their debutante daughters. Her simple diction and direct manner, even her tendency to diffuseness, were all apt to the writing of fables for, like La Fontaine, she wished to adorn a tale as well as to point a moral. She adapts her sources, as La Fontaine had done, with much freedom, and provides familiar English detail in place of the exotic. Sometimes she makes a change to improve the didactic purpose, as when she replaces La Fontaine's bumpkin in *Le Gland et la citrouille* with an atheist, whom she would rather deride. Or she will insert some quiet aside from her own experience as in *The Eagle, the Sow and the Cat*, after describing the stately oak which the three inhabit :

> *Thus Palaces are crammed from roof to ground,*
> *And animals as various in them found.*

Her experience of Court life was the same as that of the Elizabethans, and, like them, she constantly compares its corruption and sycophancy with the life of the country. She now seldom uses the pastoral mode, as they did, but prefers the more direct and personal comment of one who, after a Revolution which had given every opportunity to timeservers, had removed from Court to country house. La Fontaine's fable of *Le Meunier, son, fils, et l'âne* naturally therefore finds a place among those which she translated. Racan invites Malherbe's advice :

> *Tell me, how I my course of life shall shape :*
> *To something I would fix ere 't be too late.*
> *You know my birth, my talents, my estate :*
> *Shall I, with thee, content, all search resign*
> *And to the country my desires confine ?*

Malherbe's advice in the fable is that whatever we do is certain to lie open to criticism, and that the only sensible course is to follow one's own mind. Certainly this was Lady Winchilsea's custom, and the criticism she resented was the patronizing criticism that was based not on her merits as a poet but on her sex : 'Women' (she said) 'are Education's and not Nature's fools.' Recognizing no need to apologize for her sex she never attempted to compete with masculine writers, but made her poems out of her own feminine experience. Her mock-heroic parody of Milton, *Fanscomb Barn*, derides the pompous imitations of a great poet, not the poet himself. She had too precise a self-knowledge ever to risk such a comparison.

The fables form a large part of the volume which she eventually published in 1713, and are more likely than most of her poems to have been written with such a book in mind. She introduced the collection, *Miscellany Poems*, with what she called a prefatory fable, *Mercury and the Elephant*, freely adapted from La Fontaine's *L'Eléphant et le singe de Jupiter* which she applies to herself, to show how little expectation she had of any notice from the critics. But she would never admit that there was anything unfeminine in writing poetry :

> *Why should it in my pen be held a fault,*
> *Whilst Mira paints her face, to paint a thought ?*

Most important of all, her husband approved not only of her writing poems, but of her publishing them too. In his will he expressed his approval of his executors 'reprinting all my dear wife's poems which have been already published, with the addition of all the rest of her finished poems which are yet in manuscript . . . And this is what I would see performed myself, if it shall please God to spare my life.' Her book was published anonymously though some copies had her name printed on the title-page without her authority. However, as Lord Winchilsea said in a letter written the following year, 'all the town knew her to be the author of it'.

She was by nature a private, retiring person, not eager for the kind of public position which any author must accept. She resented the attribution to her of satires which she had not written, and perhaps still more the calumny spread at Tunbridge Wells that she was indifferent to music. But she kept her good humour and inserted a poetical *Advertisement* in three journals of the day.

> *Whereas 'tis spread about the town*
> *That I, a person of renown,*

Have yet in harmony no taste
With which the British land is graced,
This is to certify the wrong
Is done me by some lessening tongue
Which I resolve to bear no longer.

and so on for more than a hundred Hudibrastic lines, which suggest that she was quite amused to find herself 'a person of renown'.

Already, before her book's publication, she was known as a poet. Rowe and Swift had printed complimentary poetic addresses to her, Swift's poem *Apollo Outwitted* coming out in his *Miscellanies in Prose and Verse* of 1711. At the time when he wrote she still had no thought of publishing her poems, for the point of his poem is that Ardelia had outwitted Apollo by winning from him the gift of poetry without making any return, and for this the god had determined to punish the lady with modesty such that her gift would remain for ever unknown. This may have been Swift's method of encouraging her to print, but in any event he would have been able at once to identify the authoress of *Miscellany Poems*, and he would be likely to commend them to his literary friends in London. Among these would be Pope; and Lady Winchilsea, more confident in her social position than in her status as a newly-fledged poet, invited him to dinner towards the end of the year. She then inflicted upon him a reading of her early play *Love and Innocence*, and Pope 'seized and tied down to judge' confessed afterwards that the occasion, at least so far as he was concerned, had not been a great success. However, next year Pope addressed to her a most flattering *Impromptu* in reply to her protest against his satire on female authors in *The Rape of the Lock* :

In vain you boast poetic names of yore,
And cite those Sapphos we admire no more :
Fate doomed the fall of every female wit,
But doomed it then when first Ardelia writ,

because she had so far surpassed all her predecessors. To this she replied with some delightful verses, reminding Pope of Orpheus' fate at women's hands, though he need not fear his awkward fate,

The lock won't cost the head,

which suggest that, whatever the frigidities of that first dinner party, a happy intimacy had ensued. And when Pope's collected *Works* appeared in 1717 a complimentary poem by Lady Winchilsea preceded it, which was reprinted in later editions after her death. There seems therefore good reason for believing that Pope, whatever his general opinion of Female Wits, enjoyed the company both of Lady Winchilsea and of her verses.

Pope's praise of her helped to maintain the reputation of her poetry during the half century after her death in 1720. *The Spleen* remained her most admired poem, but the fables also were still in fashion. Anna Seward, the celebrated blue-stocking of Lichfield whose scepticism about ghosts shocked Dr Johnson, had learnt at her mother's knee, though without knowing the name of the author, Lady Winchilsea's poem *Life's Progress*. But there is nothing to show that William Cowper, whose own sureness of touch in writing of the domestic scene often recalls Lady Winchilsea's similar tact, had ever read her poems which he would, surely, have enjoyed.

Thus it was left to Wordsworth to revive the fame of a poet whom Pope had once admired. This paradox derives

from their preference for different parts of her work. Wordsworth thought that 'she was unlucky in her models, Pin-
daric Odes and French Fables', and though he approved
two of the fables, *Love, Death and Reputation* and *The Shepherd and the Calm*, he had no very high opinion of *The Spleen*,
which was even in his day better known than any other of
her poems. Pope could admire in her Augustan qualities,
even if he would have rejected her fondness for triplets and
alexandrines, and her excessive use of low monosyllables,
whereas Wordsworth discovered in her a poet of Romantic
sensibility, whose un-Augustan liking for monosyllables suggested that she preferred 'a selection of the language really
used by men'. Her style, he says, 'is chaste, tender, and
vigorous, and entirely free from sparkle, antithesis, and that
over-culture, which reminds one by its broad glare, its stiff-
ness, and heaviness, of the double daisies of the garden,
compared with their modest and sensitive kindred of the
fields'. Lady Winchilsea might have demurred at some
parts of this flattery, since she was not averse from antithesis
on occasion, and enjoyed both garden flowers and wild
flowers ; nor would she readily have attributed modest
sensitivity to a daisy. But Wordsworth saw that she was the
sort of poet whose 'eye had been steadily fixed upon her
object', and whose feelings had urged her to work upon it in
the spirit of genuine imagination'. Above all he found in
her a poet whose enjoyment of the countryside derived, like
his own, from long familiarity with it.

He first mentioned her in 1815, in the *Essay, Supple-
mentary to the Preface* where he named her *Nocturnal Reverie* as
one of the very few poems between *Paradise Lost* and *The
Seasons* to contain new images of external nature. Five years
later he made a private anthology of poems to send to Lady
Mary Lowther as a Christmas present. Of the fifty poems

transcribed no less than seventeen were by Lady Winchilsea
and, even if we allow that Wordsworth may have thought
poems by one aristocratic lady a suitable gift to another, the
choice of so many denotes his partiality. His interest continued, and ten years later he had some correspondence on
the subject of her poems with Dyce, who had included four
in his *Specimens of British Poetesses*, 1825. Among Dyce's
selection were two of Wordsworth's favourites, *Life's Progress* (the poem Anna Seward had by heart) and *A Nocturnal
Reverie*.

This poem uses the phrase 'In such a night' with the same
incantatory effect as Lorenzo and Jessica use it in their
exquisite dialogue in the fifth act of *The Merchant of Venice* ;
it can easily support the comparison it invites. For
whereas Lorenzo and Jessica use the phrase to call up
memories of classical lovers in order to lead on with delicate
wit to their own confessions of love, Lady Winchilsea is
concerned only with

> *The short-lived jubilee the creatures keep,*
> *Which but endures whilst tyrant man does sleep.*

She conveys the listening stillness of night in the country,
with its succession of unrelated and sometimes puzzling
sounds,

> *When the loosed horse now, as his pasture leads*
> *Comes slowly grazing through the adjoining meads,*
> *Whose stealing pace and lengthened shade we fear,*
> *Till torn-up forage in his teeth we hear.*

She notes too the faded colours of flowers by moonlight, and
their increased scents. And in a very Wordsworthian passage she draws the moral of her reverie :

But silent musings urge the mind to seek
Something too high for syllables to speak ;
Till the free soul to a composedness charmed,
Finding the elements of rage disarmed,
O'er all below a solemn quiet grown,
Joys in the inferior world, and thinks it like her own.

Wordsworth did not make the mistake of admiring her poetry only when it seemed like an anticipation of his own. He enjoyed those poems in which she revealed her own very different nature, such as *The Critic and the Writer of Fables*, where she parodies various current forms with a gaiety quite foreign to his poetry ; or *A Tale of the Miser and the Poet*, where she gives a lively account of contemporary poets and their misfortunes. He admired her elegy on James Thynne for its personal sincerity of feeling, and, more unexpectedly (because for the opposite reason, that she could write well when her personal feelings were not concerned) the *Description of a Tapestry at Longleat*. Thus he could delight both in her public and in her private poems, even, despite his distaste for the forms, in Pindarick Ode and Fable and heroic couplet, for she provided three things which he looked for in poetry: personal self-revelation, careful observation of the natural world, and a serious morality, and all expressed without affectation or obvious artifice. Perhaps in her clear self-knowledge she came closest to Wordsworth at his best. But whereas he wrote with the inspiration that he was writing for mankind, and when that failed wrote unworthily, Lady Winchilsea wrote for friends who shared her tastes and enjoyed her hospitality. She restricted herself to the world she knew, and wrote always within her range. Wordsworth's appreciation of poetry that is in many ways so unlike his own, but yet often strangely foreshadows something of his style and sensibility, is no aberration of taste. And if it is the most distinguished compliment ever paid to her poetry, it is by no means more than she deserved.

When she died, in August 1720, she was away in London, but she was brought home for burial in the little church at Eastwell where she had worshipped for so long. Six years later Lord Winchilsea was buried beside her, and among his ancestors of two centuries. During the 1939–1945 war the church was so damaged through vibration from anti-aircraft guns sited close by that a few years later it collapsed. Both their tombs were destroyed.

TEXTS

No complete edition of Lady Winchilsea's poems has yet been published. The best edition, long out of print, is that edited by Myra Reynolds, Chicago, 1903. The only selection in print is in H. I'A. Fausset's *Minor Poets of the Eighteenth Century*, Dent, 1930 (Everyman's Library). This reprints 89 poems.

INDEX

Catherine of Braganza, Queen, 97, 130
Catullus, 120
Cavendish, Catherine, *see* Thanet,
    Countess of
Chantilly, 19
Charles I, 102, 105, 113, 118, 121, 141
Charles II, 87, 91, 97, 100, 102, 113–14,
    120–1, 130, 140, 144, 147
Charles V, Emperor, 8, 9, 15
Chatsworth, Derbys., 154–5
Chaucer, Geoffrey, 16, 18, 34, 53, 62,
    75, 82, 90, 92
Chesterfield, Philip, 2nd Earl of, 148–9,
    151
Cholmondeley, Francis, 144
Christina, Queen of Sweden, 129
Churchyard, Thomas, 57, 60
Clarendon, Edward, 1st Earl of, 100,
    139–40, 147
Clere, Thomas, 28, 31
Clifford, Arthur, 110
Clifford Chambers, Glos. (now
    Warws.), 69, 85
Cobham, Thomas, 8th Lord, 4
Cokayne, Sir Aston, 139, 141–3, 150
Coleridge, Samuel Taylor, 30, 68, 135
Coleshill Manor, Herts. (now Bucks.),
    87
Colton Hall, Staffs., 109
Congreve, William, 167, 173
Constable, John, 138
Corneille, Pierre, 141
Cornish, William, 4
Cotton, Beresford, 147, 149–50
Cotton, Cassandra, 144
Cotton, Charles, the elder, 138–41,
    144, 147–8, 150, 152
Cotton, Charles, the younger, 107,
    109, 133–56 *passim*
Cotton, Isabella, *see* Hutchinson,
    Isabella
Cotton, Olive, 139–40, 152
Cowdray Park, Sussex, 41
Cowley, Abraham, 89, 148, 173
Cowper, William, 179
Cromwell, Oliver, 87, 100, 104, 121,
    130, 142, 149, 153, 164
cross-rhyme, 39, 115
Croxall, Staffs., 66
Curzon, Mary, 66

Dacier, André, 175

Daniel, Samuel, 27, 70, 72–74, 108, 111,
    126
Dante, 21
Darrell, Elizabeth, 8
Davenant, Sir William, 89, 97, 138
Denham, Sir John, 118, 124, 143, 163
Derby, James, 7th Earl of, 143
Dolce, Lodovico, 40
Donne, John, 29, 45, 65, 76, 81, 84, 85,
    94, 108–9, 138–9, 156
Dormer, Mary, 41
Dormer, Robert, 41
Douglas, Gavin, 23, 24
Douglas, Margaret, 6, 34
Dowland, John, 14
Drayton, Michael, 20, 27, 57, 59–86
    passim, 88, 108, 111, 126, 139
Dryden, John, 21–23, 25, 45, 55, 76, 77,
    85, 87, 88, 90, 92, 116, 143, 157, 167,
    172, 175
du Vaix, Guillaume(*properly*, du Vair), 141
Dyce, Alexander, 181
Dymock, —, 117

Eastwell Park, Kent, 159, 161–3, 165,
    168, 170, 183
elegy, 30–31, 33, 62, 139, 144, 146, 182
Eliot, T. S., 91
Elizabeth I, Queen, 36, 37, 51, 52, 55,
    56, 61, 66, 81
Ellis, Sir Henry, 150
Elton, Oliver, 77
Elvaston Castle, Derbys., 139
epistolary style, *see* plain style
Erasmus, 49
Etherege, Sir George, 167
Euripides, 40
Eusden, Laurence, 169–70
Evelyn, John, 97

fable, 175–7, 180, 182
Fairfax, Edward, 75
Fairfax, Robert, 4
Fairfax, Thomas, 3rd Lord, 163–4
Falkland, Lucius, 2nd Viscount, 3, 92,
    97, 98
Fallodon, Northumb., 3
Fanshawe, Anne (wife of Sir Richard),
    105, 111, 113–14, 121, 124, 126, 130–1
Fanshawe, Elizabeth (wife of Sir
    Henry), 102–3, 108

PRINTED BY R. & R. CLARK, LTD., EDINBURGH